DATE DUE

COMPREHENSIVE RESEARCH
AND STUDY GUIDE

BLOOM'S
MAJOR
SHORT STORY
WRITERS

John

Updike

EDITED AND WITH AN
INTRODUCTION BY HAROLD BLOOM

BLOOM'S MAJOR
SHORT STORY
WRITERS
Anton Chekhov
Joseph Conrad
Stephen Crane
William Faulkner
F. Scott Fitzgerald
Nathaniel Hawthorne
Ernest Hemingway
O. Henry
Shirley Jackson
Henry James
James Joyce
D. H. Lawrence
Jack London
Herman Melville
Flannery O'Connor
Edgar Allan Poe
Katherine Anne Porter
J. D. Salinger
John Steinbeck
Mark Twain
John Updike
Eudora Welty

BLOOM'S MAJOR
WORLD POETS
Maya Angelou
Robert Browning
Geoffrey Chaucer
Samuel T. Coleridge
Dante
Emily Dickinson
John Donne
T. S. Eliot
Robert Frost
Homer
Langston Hughes
John Keats
John Milton
Sylvia Plath
Edgar Allan Poe
Poets of World War I
Shakespeare's Poems
  & Sonnets
Percy Shelley
Alfred, Lord Tennyson
Walt Whitman
William Wordsworth
William Butler Yeats

COMPREHENSIVE RESEARCH
AND STUDY GUIDE

BLOOM'S MAJOR SHORT STORY WRITERS

John

Updike

EDITED AND WIT

© 2001 by Chelsea House Publishers, a subsidiary of
Haights Cross Communications.

Introduction © 2001 by Harold Bloom.

Printed and bound in the United States of America.

First Printing
1 3 5 7 9 8 6 4 2

Library of Congress Cataloging-in-Publication Data
John Updike / Harold Bloom, ed.
    p. cm. — (Bloom's major short story writers)
    Includes bibliographical references and index.
    ISBN 0-7910-5946-4 (alk. paper)
    1. Updike, John—Criticism and interpretation—Handbooks, manuals,
  etc. 2. Updike, John—Examinations—Study guides. 3. Short story—
Examinations—Study guides. 4. Short story—Handbooks, manuals, etc.
I. Bloom, Harold. II. Series.
PS3571.P4 Z73 2000
813'.54—dc21   00-038397
                                                      CIP

Chelsea House Publishers
1974 Sproul Road, Suite 400
Broomall, PA 19008-0914

The Chelsea House World Wide Web address is
http://www.chelseahouse.com

Contributing Editor: Elizabeth Beaudin

Produced by: Robert Gerson Publisher's Services, Avondale, PA

Contents

User's Guide

This volume is designed to present biographical, critical, and bibliographical information on the author's best-known or most important short stories. Following Harold Bloom's editor's note and introduction is a detailed biography of the author, discussing major life events and important literary accomplishments. A plot summary of each short story follows, tracing significant themes, patterns, and motifs in the work, and an annotated list of characters supplies brief information on the main characters in each story.

A selection of critical extracts, derived from previously published material from leading critics, analyzes aspects of each short story. The extracts consist of statements from the author, if available, early reviews of the work, and later evaluations up to the present. A bibliography of the author's writings (including a complete list of all books written, cowritten, edited, and translated), a list of additional books and articles on the author and the work, and an index of themes and ideas in the author's writings conclude the volume.

∼

Harold Bloom is Sterling Professor of the Humanities at Yale University and Henry W. and Albert A. Berg Professor of English at the New York University Graduate School. He is the author of over 20 books, including *Shelley's Mythmaking* (1959), *The Visionary Company* (1961), *Blake's Apocalypse* (1963), *Yeats* (1970), *A Map of Misreading* (1975), *Kabbalah and Criticism* (1975), *Agon: Toward a Theory of Revisionism* (1982), *The American Religion* (1992), *The Western Canon* (1994), and *Omens of Millennium: The Gnosis of Angels, Dreams, and Resurrection* (1996). *The Anxiety of Influence* (1973) sets forth Professor Bloom's provocative theory of the literary relationships between the great writers and their predecessors. His most recent books include *Shakespeare: The Invention of the Human,* a 1998 National Book Award finalist, and *How to Read and Why,* which was published in 2000.

Professor Bloom earned his Ph.D. from Yale University in 1955 and has served on the Yale faculty since then. He is a 1985 MacArthur Foundation Award recipient, served as the Charles Eliot Norton Professor of Poetry at Harvard University in 1987–88, and has received honorary degrees from the universities of Rome and Bologna. In 1999, Professor Bloom received the prestigious American Academy of Arts and Letters Gold Medal for Criticism.

Currently, Harold Bloom is the editor of numerous Chelsea House volumes of literary criticism, including the series BLOOM'S NOTES, BLOOM'S MAJOR DRAMATISTS, BLOOM'S MAJOR NOVELISTS, MAJOR LITERARY CHARACTERS, MODERN CRITICAL VIEWS, MODERN CRITICAL INTERPRETATIONS, and WOMEN WRITERS OF ENGLISH AND THEIR WORKS.

Editor's Note

This volume confines itself to five of John Updike's best-known short stories. My Introduction admires the art of "A & P," certainly one of Updike's most brilliant inventions.

As there are thirty-five Critical Views extracted here, I call attention only to some that I myself find among the most useful commentaries upon Updike's stories.

"A & P," which may be Updike's masterpiece in the short-story form, is compared by Patrick W. Shaw to Hawthorne's "Young Goodman Brown," and by Walter Wells to James Joyce's "Araby."

"Ace in the Hole," a beautifully melancholy vignette, acquires particular resonance from Charlie Reilly's reading, which finds in "Ace" the source for *Rabbit, Run,* one of Updike's major novels.

Jay Cantor and Updike himself meditate upon the rhetoric of "Flight," after which the famous "Pigeon Feathers" is illuminated by the late Arthur Mizener and by Updike himself.

The remarkably titled "Packed Dirt, Churchgoing, A Dying Cat, A Traded Car" is a story that tends to divide its readers. Jane Barnes questions Updike's moral grasp in this story, while Robert M. Luscher finds "a conscious thematic and imagistic logic."

Introduction

HAROLD BLOOM

John Updike is a major stylist, whose literary production has been vast and varied. He may be most himself in his short stories, where style itself can constitute a mode of vision. No novel by Updike persuades me as fully as do stories like "A & P" and "Pigeon Feathers," if only because the novelist so overtly contaminates his principal longer narratives with his own beliefs and opinions. Frequently, these judgments and views are of considerable interest in themselves, but they can distract the reader's attention from persons, places, and events.

In "A & P" there are no distractions, and Updike's art is as subtle as Joyce's in *Dubliners*. Sammy, nineteen and very limited in education and social understanding, falls into a passion for "Queenie," a young beauty who never will be available to someone of his social class. He makes the Quixotic gesture of quitting his job at the A & P, though "Queenie" never will know that he has protested against her embarrassment by the store manager. Updike deftly conveys that Sammy's action is more a pose than a gesture, though Sammy says: "it seems to me that once you begin a gesture it's fatal not to go through with it."

The sad reality is that gestures are for those who can afford them, and Sammy cannot. Updike accurately can be praised for profound social insight in "A & P," but the story, like Joyce's "Two Gallants" or "Araby," is imaginatively richer than social understanding tends to be by itself. In less than half-a-dozen pages, Updike condenses a life, up to its nineteenth year, and also intimates how unlikely that life is to develop in any way that might satisfy its dream of erotic fulfillment. The economy of "A & P," and its consistent verbal rightness, testify to a superb artist in the short-story form. ❀

Biography of
John Updike

John Hoyer Updike was born in Reading, Pennsylvania, on March 18, 1932, the son of Linda Grace Hoyer and Wesley Russell Updike. His mother aspired to be a writer, and his father was a mathematics teacher at the local junior high school. For the first thirteen years of his life, Updike lived at 117 Philadelphia Avenue in Shillington, Pennsylvania (this town would become the basis for Updike's fictional town of Olinger). When John was thirteen, his family moved a few miles away to Plowville, returning to the farm where his mother was raised.

At Shillington High School, Updike contributed articles, poems, and drawings to the school newspaper. In his yearbook, his profile mentions that "the sage of Plowville hopes to write for a living." Once out of high school, Updike worked as a copy boy for the *Reading Eagle* before he entered Harvard College on a full scholarship. While at Harvard, John Updike worked on the *Harvard Lampoon,* first as a cartoonist, later as a writer of poems and prose, and finally as its president.

While still at Harvard, on June 26, 1953, Updike married Mary Pennington, a student at Radcliffe College and the daughter of a Unitarian minister. A year later, Updike graduated *summa cum laude* from Harvard College. About the same time, the *New Yorker* purchased from Updike a story, "Friends from Philadelphia," and a poem, "Duet, with Muffled Brake Drums." The following academic year, Updike studied at the Ruskin School of Drawing and Fine Art in Oxford, England, on a Knox Fellowship. While still in England, he met E. B. White from the *New Yorker,* who offered Updike a staff post on the prestigious magazine. Updike had always dreamed of writing for the *New Yorker*; he and his wife returned to the United States and settled down in New York City.

During the years 1955 to 1957, Updike's first two children, Elizabeth and David, were born. Meanwhile, big-city life was proving to be too expensive and overwhelming for Updike. In a *New York Times* interview, Updike remarked about the city, "The trouble with living here is that nothing seems important." In March of 1957, Updike quit his *New Yorker* job to relocate his family to Ipswich, Massachusetts, so that he could focus his attention on his fiction and his poems.

Ipswich was not so different from Shillington, Updike's boyhood home. The small-town atmosphere allowed Updike to experience the ordinary, middle-class life that would become the central subject of much of his work. Unlike other literary figures, Updike had no interest either in isolating himself from the rest of humanity, or in participating in an elite, literary society. Instead, he and his wife found a sense of belonging in the small-town middle class, and in Ipswich, he wrote *The Poorhouse Fair*, his first novel. In 1958, Harper and Brothers published his first book, *The Carpentered Hen and Other Tame Creatures*.

The next year was eventful for Updike: his son Michael was born; Updike changed publishers, from Harper and Brothers to Alfred A. Knopf, so that *The Poorhouse Fair* would be published with the ending he wanted; and that same year Knopf also published *The Same Door*, Updike's first collection of short stories. He also won a John Simon Guggenheim Foundation grant that enabled him to begin work on what became his best-known novel, *Rabbit, Run*.

In 1960, his daughter Miranda was born, *Rabbit, Run* was published, and Updike won the Rosenthal Award from the National Institute of Arts and Letters for *The Poorhouse Fair*. In the years that followed, Updike wrote *The Centaur* (1963), for which he won the National Book Award for Fiction. He was elected to the American Academy of Arts and Sciences and received the first O. Henry Prize for his short story "The Bulgarian Poetess" in 1966.

These years in Updike's career are often called his "Pennsylvania Period," because his fiction re-created his childhood home. However, in 1968, Updike broke away from his earlier work with *Couples*, a novel set in a small New England town. This book, Updike's first best-seller, landed him on the cover of *Time* magazine.

Updike's success continued in the seventies with the appearance of *Bech: A Book* (1970)—the first in the Bech series, a character some critics consider Updike's alter ego. The same year, *Rabbit, Run* was made into a movie; while in the following year, 1971, Updike published *Rabbit Redux*.

Personally, Updike was not as fortunate. In 1974, he separated from his wife Mary and filed for divorce two years later. In the meantime, however, his career continued to move ahead: Updike published the first in his *Scarlet Letter* trilogy, *A Month of Sundays*. When his divorce was final in 1975, Updike married Martha Bernhard.

In 1978, Updike's novel, *The Coup*, received good reviews, as it was greeted as a departure from the established suburban setting in Updike's earlier works. Set in a fictional African country, this book demonstrated that Updike's imaginative vision was powerful enough to look beyond small-town America. Inspired by this success and his new marriage, Updike wrote some of his finest fiction during these years.

In the eighties, Updike's literary fortune prospered. First, his short story "The Music School" was produced for public television in 1980 as part of the "American Short Story" series. Updike then received the Edward MacDowell Medal for Literature in 1981. That same year Updike's *Rabbit Is Rich* was published; this book garnered him the National Book Critics Circle Award for Fiction. The following year, Updike won both the Pulitzer Prize and the American Book Award for this novel. To commemorate Updike's fiftieth birthday, Alfred A. Knopf reissued *The Carpentered Hen*, Updike's first book. That same year, Updike also published *Bech Is Back*. In 1984, he received the National Book Critics Circle Award for Criticism for *Hugging the Shore*. Updike also won the National Arts Club Medal of Honor that year. As prolific as ever, he published *The Witches of Eastwick* in 1984. This novel was made into a movie two years later. In 1986, the second book in the *Scarlet Letter* trilogy, *Roger's Version*, was published. The third book in the series, *S.*, was finished in 1988. That same year Updike delivered the first Annual PEN/Malamud Memorial Reading at the Folger Shakespeare Library in Washington, D.C. The decade ended with more accolades for Updike when he was awarded the National Medal of Arts from then-president George Bush.

In 1990, Updike published the last novel in the Harry Angstrom series, *Rabbit at Rest*. The next year Updike won both the National Book Critics Circle Award and a second Pulitzer Prize for this novel. In 1991, Updike was also a repeat winner of the O. Henry Prize for his short story "A Sandstone Farmhouse." He earned the Conch Republic Prize for Literature in 1993.

As the 21st century begins, John Updike continues to write and publish. His first novel published in the new millenium is entitled *Gertrude and Claudius*. With nearly 50 books to his credit, he has created a diverse body of work that testifies to the breadth of his ability, as well as the tireless dedication he brings to bear upon that talent. ❀

Plot Summary of
"A & P"

Part of the collection of narratives in *Pigeon Feathers and Other Stories*, "A & P" was first published in the *New Yorker* on July 22, 1961.

On a typically uneventful Thursday afternoon, Sammy, a 19-year-old cashier at the local A & P, sees something unusual: "In walks these three girls in nothing but bathing suits." As he turns his complete attention to the first one in a "plaid green two-piece," Sammy is so distracted that he incurs the complaints of an older female customer, whom he describes as "a witch about fifty with rouge on her cheekbones and no eyebrows." Sammy finishes up with the unpleasant lady in time to see all three girls coming back toward the checkout lanes.

He considers the first two—the chunky one in the plaid two-piece and her companion, a tall girl with unruly black hair—but then his attention turns to the third girl, and he concludes: "She was the queen. She kind of led them, the other two peeking around and making their shoulders round. She didn't look around, not this queen, she just walked straight on slowly, on these long white prima-donna legs." His assessment clearly reflects an adolescent male outlook: "You never know for sure how girls' minds work (do you really think it's a mind in there or just a little buzz like a bee in a glass jar?) but you got the idea she had talked the other two into coming in here with her, and now she was showing them how to do it, walk slow and hold yourself straight." Sammy's further description of her bathing suit implies that in his view the suit isn't half as important as the glimpse of her skin it permits: "With the straps pushed off, there was nothing between the top of the suit and the top of her head except just her . . ."

Sammy senses that she knows she is being observed by both him and his coworker Stokesie. To his increasing amazement, the girl doesn't flinch under this scrutiny. Rather, she leads her two companions through the aisles, causing a stir among the customers as well. Sammy's thoughts sum up the impact of the girls' presence on those in the A & P: "You know, it's one thing to have a girl in a bathing suit down on the beach, where what with the glare nobody can look at each other much anyway, and another thing in the cool of the A & P, under the fluorescent lights . . . with her feet paddling naked over our checker-board green-and-cream rubber-tile floor." He and Stokesie exchange cryptic yet knowing comments. Sammy respects Stokesie's remarks, because, after all, Stokesie, though a mere three years Sammy's senior, already had "two babies chalked up on his fuselage." Again, Sammy gives us insight into the spectacle caused by the girls, explaining that the A & P, situated in a beach community, has a direct view of "two banks and the Congregational church and three real-estate offices . . ." The store is, in other words, in the heart of respectability.

As Sammy describes it, a Thursday afternoon at the A & P is a slow time that offers ample opportunity for fantasizing over such a rare event as the girls' appearance. He wonders from which aisle in the pinball-like floor plan of the store the girls will emerge. As they appear and drift toward his register, Sammy cannot be sure that "Queenie," his private nickname for his favorite girl, carries any money for her purchase until, "Still with that prim look she lifts a folded dollar bill out of the hollow at the center of her nubbed pink top."

His reverie is interrupted, however, by the appearance of the store manager. Mr. Lengel changes the tone of the scene with a heavy hand, insisting loudly that the girls be decently dressed when they enter the A & P. From Sammy's perspective, Lengel's harangue goes too far when "Queenie" appears to blush at the rebukes. Lengel, however, thinks he had made his point when he announces: "Girls, I don't want to argue with you. After this come in here with your shoulders covered. It's our policy."

During the debate, the other customers in the store herd together like sheep. Sammy, though, takes offense at Lengel's attitude, and he decides to become the girls' hero by quitting his job. The girls leave the store, apparently unaware of Sammy's sacrifice, but Sammy nevertheless informs Lengel that his decision to quit is final. Outwardly steadfast, as Sammy exits he inwardly reflects that "my stomach kind of fell as I felt how hard the world was going to be to me hereafter." ❀

List of Characters in
"A & P"

Sammy is a 19-year-old cashier at the A & P in a town close to the beach. He wakes from the monotony of his job when three teenage girls enter the store. He is smitten by one of the girls in particular and quits his job when the store manager insults her. Sammy provides a thorough description of the three girls as well as analysis of the effect they have on the sheep-like customers in the store.

Lengel is the strident manager for whom Sammy works; he enforces a store dress code that ensures that the A & P's customers dress decently.

Stokesie is another cashier in the store; this 22-year-old is married and the father of two.

McMahon is the meat counter man who waits on Queenie. He observes the girl's physical characteristics closely.

"Plaid" is the nickname Sammy uses for this chunky girl because of the two-piece bathing suit she wears.

"Big Tall Goony-Goony" is the second of the female trio that catches Sammy's eye; she has black hair that hasn't quite frizzed right, according to Sammy.

"Queenie," in Sammy's opinion, is the leader of the threesome; she both inspires him to have lustful thoughts and to challenge Lengel's provincial attitude. Queenie carries herself differently than her two companions. She seems surer of herself; in Sammy's mind, this self-confidence increases her appeal. ❀

Critical Views on
"A & P"

JANET OVERMYER ON COURTLY LOVE

[Janet Overmyer has also written on e. e. cummings and F. Scott Fitzgerald. In this early essay on Updike's frequently anthologized tale, Overmyer maintains that Updike is following the model of courtly love in his narrative by placing Sammy in the role of the humble lover who sacrifices everything for his untouchable love interest. One proof for this hypothesis is the nickname that Sammy gives his "lady": "Queenie." His description of her beauty and her demeanor places Queenie above all others.]

Updike seems to be setting up a poignant, gently teasing parallel of the medieval theme of courtly love, exemplified by the humble lover who performs noble deeds for the haughty, aristocratic lady who is so far above him as to be untouchable.

The nickname Sammy gives the seeming leader, Queenie, prepares for her elevated status, as do the details of her appearance: "long white prima-donna legs," "she held her head so high her neck . . . looked kind of stretched," "she had talked the other two into coming in here with her and now she was showing them how to do it, walk slow and hold yourself straight." Her bathing suit top is down and has slipped enough to reveal a "shining rim" around the edges.

Contrasted with her are not only her companions—a "chunky one" with a pale belly, and one "with black hair that hadn't quite frizzed right" and a "chin that was too long"—but the other women Sammy notices or remembers: a cash-register witch of about fifty, "women with six children and varicose veins," a young married woman screaming at her children, and the "sheep pushing their carts down the aisle." Queenie's superiority is obvious.

—Janet Overmyer, "Courtly Love in the A & P," *Notes on Contemporary Literature* 2, no. 3 (May 1972): p. 4.

[In this essay, M. Gilbert Porter, who has also studied the works of Sinclair Lewis and Saul Bellow, discusses Sammy's relationship with the store manager, Lengel, to defend his own description of Sammy as an Emersonian non-conformist. As manager of the store, Lengel clearly represents the Establishment that Sammy must buck in order to affirm his support of the girls' rights to dress as they like.]

According to Sammy, Lengel is "pretty dreary," but this capsuled evaluation is rendered even harsher by the implications of Sammy's metaphorical description of the manager: Lengel, Sammy reports, has been "haggling with a truck full of cabbages" (suggesting a fishwife) before he comes in and confronts the girls; it is his usual habit to "scuttle" (like a beetle) into the office behind the door "marked MANAGER," where he "hides all day" (like a rat). As a close friend of Sammy's family, Lengel carries some parental authority; as a teacher in the Sunday school, he is a voice in the church; as the MANAGER of the A&P, he is a voice in the business community. In short, Lengel represents the Voice of The Establishment. As one of the "kingpins" who enforce "policy," he sees himself as the voice of authority, the guardian of the community ethic. Sammy even imagines Lengel "thinking all these years the A&P was a great big dune and he was the head lifeguard." In this role, then, and with his "sad Sunday-school-superintendent stare" (which equates flesh with sin), he delivers in the name of decency his pious judgment to the girls: "After this come in here with your shoulders covered. It's our policy." Asserting that they "*are* decent," Queenie leads her friends indignantly from the store.

Sammy, upon whom the issues underlying the incident have forced a decision, declares his intention to "quit." His gesture is both an affirmation of the girls' decency and a rejection of the A&P and the misplaced values for which it stands. That his act is a little histrionic results from his adolescence; it does not detract from the basic nobility of his chivalric intent, nor does it reduce the magnitude of his personal commitment. As Sammy prepares to leave, however, Lengel makes a final pitch for The Establishment. "You'll feel this," he warns, "for the rest of your life." But Sammy is not buying Lengel's line: He punches the "No Sale tab" and walks outside, where "the sunshine is skating around on the asphalt."

Sammy knows that Lengel's prediction is true. As he looks back into the store, he sees Lengel "checking the sheep through" and realizes that the world is going to be hard on him "hereafter." He is aware, of course, that he has separated himself from the flock, from the "A&P crowd," and has chosen to set himself against the majority—to incur that wrath which Emerson declared was the lot of the nonconformist.

—M. Gilbert Porter, "John Updike's 'A & P': The Establishment and an Emersonian Cashier," *English Journal* 61, no. 8 (November 1972): pp. 1157–58.

RONALD E. MCFARLAND ON "BRAND-NAME SYMBOLISM"

[The author of articles in many critical journals, Ronald E. McFarland begins his analysis of "A & P" by referring to the existing body of criticism on this narrative. As a point of departure from his colleagues, in this excerpt, McFarland presents examples of what he terms "brand-name symbolism" in Updike's story. To this end, McFarland mentions the many products that appear in the text as well as the store name itself. McFarland contends that though some of the symbols appear trivial, they point to the overall ironic quality of the tale.]

In order to illustrate (in a couple senses of the word) this story, Updike creates what I will call "brand-name symbolism." From the HiHo crackers to the Falcon station wagon, Updike's brand names are more than simply appropriate projections of the setting. They are symbols, comical, if only because of their nature and context, which have meaningful associations when properly considered. They also contribute to the ironic portraits offered throughout the story.

Sammy associates himself at the outset with HiHo crackers, and they are a fitting symbol for him—an ordinary, middle-class (not Ritz crackers) snack item. How seriously, then, ought one to take Sammy? How seriously does he take himself? The brand name connotes light-heartedness and high spirits. The movement of the story, and of Sammy's perspective, is from the easy gaiety and freedom of youth toward the "hard" realities of adult societal judgment. As Sammy observes, his parents think what has happened is "sad," but, although he sees that life hereafter will be hard for him, he doesn't yet see how unfortunate is his fall from boyhood.

The girl Sammy calls "Queenie" is associated with "Kingfish Fancy Herring Snacks in Pure Sour Cream: 49¢." (I recently priced a similar product at $1.98 for an 8-ounce jar.) The brand name not only fits the imperial Queenie, but also suggests the social class, the upper crust, to which she belongs. The incongruity of the common HiHo crackers and a luxury hors d'oeuvres like herring snacks anticipates one aspect of the hard lesson that Sammy will learn. Queenie's brand-name symbol represents a world completely alien to that of Sammy, who visualizes her parents and their stylish friends "picking up herring snacks on toothpicks off a big glass plate." As X. J. Kennedy observes in his instructor's manual, the unsophisticated Sammy "thinks martinis are garnished with mint." The brand name that Sammy refers to as symbolic of his own family is Schlitz.

In the confrontation itself there are several ironies. The A&P, after all, is the subsuming brand name in the story. It is a democratic melting pot of sorts, a typically American institution where, just as the Atlantic and Pacific come together, so do crackers and herring snacks, and so do the proletarian (the "bum" in his baggy pants who buys pineapple juice), the bourgeois, and the patrician. All are equal, one might suppose, at the supermarket. Yet it is here that a standard of social decorum is asserted, so the irony cuts at the upper class girls. Sammy is no kinder to his reflections on the proletariat (including the street-workers) and the bourgeoisie than Lengel, the manager, is in his treatment of the patricians. At the same time, the social code itself is undercut, for though it is distinctly bourgeois in nature, its aim is to sustain the appearance of "class" (the patrician). The code of decorum keeps the store from being what it would pretend to be. The supposedly elite upper class is, in fact, very casual, too casual, under the circumstances, for the snobbish middle-class manager.

—Ronald E. McFarland, "Updike and the Critics: Reflections on 'A & P,'" *Studies in Short Fiction* 20, no. 2–3 (Spring–Summer 1983): pp. 97–98.

Marjorie Hill Goss on Sammy's Moral
Development

[Marjorie Hill Goss, who has also written on Margaret
Drabble, retells here the substance of Updike's most anthologized tale to argue against Sammy's labeling as a courtly
love hero or an Emersonian non-conformist. She suggests
instead that Sammy is merely in the process of moral development, not uncommon for someone his age. According to
Goss, Sammy's actions break from typical sexist norms of
the period.]

Sammy, the checkout clerk of John Updike's short story "A & P," has
been seen as the hero of a courtly romance—a "humble lover who
performs noble deeds for the haughty, aristocratic lady"—and as an
Emersonian non-conformist, rejecting "the A & P and the misplaced values for which it stands." Fruitful as these readings are,
they are both misleading in their tacit assumption that Sammy
plays but one role. Actually, his attitude undergoes a change. To
follow this process as Sammy tells his story is to appreciate Updike's
skill at demonstrating in a short narrative how human perceptions
may widen: to see Sammy, at nineteen, taking a step forward in his
moral development. ⟨. . .⟩

It is one thing for Sammy to engage in girl-watching with
Stokesie, but it becomes another when an older co-worker joins in.
McMahon the butcher distresses Sammy as he studies the girls, "pat-
ting his mouth" and "sizing up their joints." At this point, seeing his
own meatmarket outlook virtually parodied, Sammy begins to
change. "Poor kids," he says, "I began to feel sorry for them." Adding
"they couldn't help it," he shows his budding understanding of their
predicament as objects of male scrutiny and evaluation.

Appreciative still of their physical attractions, Sammy becomes
fully conscious of the young women as thinking and feeling beings
when Lengel, the store manager, chastises them for not being
"decently dressed." While the tanned girl tries to explain that this
was just a quick trip for one item, and Queenie blushes and asserts
that she and her friends "*are* decent," Sammy is, one assumes, pon-
dering. The result is his quitting as a gesture of protest; even when
given a chance to keep his job, he remembers Queenie's discomfort
and refuses.

Sammy has come a long way in a short time. Rejecting the Lengel categorization of the young women as rule-breakers—troublesome nonconformists—he has also broken out of the even more confining viewpoint of the sexist.

—Marjorie Hill Goss, "Widening Perceptions in Updike's 'A & P,'" *Notes on Contemporary Literature* 14, no. 5 (November 1984): p. 8.

PAUL J. EMMETT ON UPDIKE'S SUBTLETY IN THE STORY

[Paul J. Emmett, who has also published critical studies on John Hawkes and Douglas Woolf, agrees with the prevailing criticism that "A & P" is different from some of Updike's more disparaged works, precisely because this short story is not superficial, although it may appear to be just that. Emmett believes that the narrator's self-doubt contributes to the misreading of the tale. In his analysis, he sees the insecurity and immaturity of the narrator as the essence of the story's strength.]

The contradiction, the apparent inconsistency in "A & P," which should make us question and re-examine, involves both the narrator's position and perspective. Is Sammy seeing things from the third checkout slot or from the first? At the start of the story he tells us, "I'm in the third checkout slot." Later he emphasizes this, "From the third slot I look straight up the aisle" and stresses the fact that he doesn't move, "there was nothing much to do except lean on the register and wait for the girls to show up again." But when the girls show up at the cash registers, Sammy says, "slots Three through Seven are unmanned and I could see [Queenie] wondering between Stokes and me." Now, the repeated mention of the third checkout slot at the start of the story forces us to see Sammy in this slot. So, we are left with the problem of deciding whose memory is faulty, Updike's or Sammy's. Is "slots Three through Seven are unmanned" carelessness or design—surface inconsequence or unsuspected subtlety?

The unexpected "unmanned" suggests that the mistake is Sammy's, that the apparent inconsistency is really his unconscious slip. Sammy remembers slot Three as *unmanned*—not, say, "empty," "closed," or "unoccupied"—because unconsciously he doubts his own manhood.

During this earlier recollection of gawking at the girls he remembered quite well where he was, but the pressures of confrontation, even in memory, make him question his maturity. And well he might, since this nineteen year old who sings with his cash register, who is impressed by 49¢ Fancy Herring snacks, who sees complete strangers as "my girls," who envisions all women as brainless, who still has his shirts ironed by his mother, and who uses phrases like "Fiddle-de-do"—is most immature. His "gesture" of quitting his job is, in fact, an immature attempt to shore up his suspect masculinity: "The girls . . . are in a hurry to get out, so I say 'I quit' to Lengel quick enough for them to hear, hoping they'll stop and watch me, their unsuspected hero."

Indeed, self-doubt resulting in overcompensation, the imaginary journey from unmanned to hero, can be seen repeatedly beneath the dancing surface of Sammy's narration. Consider just one example.

> 'Darling,' I said [to Stoksie]. 'Hold me tight.' Stoksie's married with two babies chalked up on his fuselage already, but as far as I can tell that's the only difference. He's twenty-two, and I was nineteen this April.

Here, Sammy's self-doubt, his immaturity and insecurity, is apparent in: his Darling game; his view of fertilization as the "heroic" assertion of Stoksie's—not his—masculinity; his consciousness of their age difference; and his attempt to make himself as old as possible. His resultant overcompensation is, "as far as I can tell that's the only difference."

But even in the compensation, his insecurity is maintained with "as far as I can tell," and this duality is also found in our original passage. Since "Stoksie [is] in the second slot" and next to Sammy, we can see that the insecurity reflected in "slots Three through Seven are unmanned" is compensated for by Sammy's imagining himself in the first slot. Again, this slip is characteristic: Sammy longs to see himself as number one. To Sammy the regular shoppers are "sheep"; someone who buys pineapple juice is a "bum"; housewives are "houseslaves"; women are brainless; and laborers are "freeloaders"; but Sammy himself—he's the "unsuspected hero."

—Paul J. Emmett, "A Slip That Shows Updike's 'A & P,'" *Notes on Contemporary Literature* 15, no. 2 (March 1985): pp. 9–10.

ALICE HALL PETRY ON CLOTHING IN THE STORY

[Alice Hall Petry has published on both 19th- and 20th-century American literature and has edited several compilations of critical essays. In this essay, Petry focuses on the references to clothing in Updike's story.]

The opening sentence is a grabber: "In walks these three girls in *nothing but* bathing suits" (emphasis added). The "nothing but"—carefully placed before "bathing suits"—jolts the reader in the same way that the three girls jolt Sammy and the supermarket patrons: the girls seem almost naked, and it is this "au naturel" quality which throughout the story will be juxtaposed against the confinement and artificiality of the A & P. Even their bathing suits seem insistently natural. The first girl Sammy notices ("a chunky kid") wears a "plaid green two-piece." Green, of course, is the color most readily associated with the natural world, and the plaid design, however unflattering, would be naturally appropriate for a "chunky" person: the boxy pattern is in keeping with her somatotype. The only other bathing suit described is Queenie's: "She had on a kind of dirty-pink—beige maybe, I don't know—bathing suit with a little nubble all over it. . . ." The "beige maybe, I don't know" imparts a hesitancy which ill-conceals what Sammy is really thinking: the suit is flesh-colored, thereby making Queenie seem even more naked than if she were wearing, say, a black bathing suit. Further, the "little nubble all over it" betokens what any naked girl might exhibit: goose-bumps. Other details about Queenie also are insistently natural: she is barefoot; "her hands are empty, not a ring or a bracelet, bare as God made them"; her "unraveling" bun of "oaky hair" had been bleached by "sun and salt"; and she stores her dollar in "the hollow at the center of her nubbled pink top"—as pristine a billfold as Adam's fingers were his "fork." But what really captures Sammy's attention about Queenie is that her bathing suit straps are not in place: ". . . what got me, the straps were down. They were off her shoulders. . . ." In part, of course, he is responding to her erotically, as the flesh-colored suit seems literally to be falling off her body ("there was nothing between the top of the suit and the top of her head except just *her*"), but Updike is careful to have Sammy be enthralled that the straps are "off her shoulders." This seemingly incidental remark takes on significance in the course of the story. Lengel the manager never states that "bathing suits are not to be worn in the A & P." Rather, he says, "'Girls, I don't want to argue with you. After this come in here with your shoulders covered. It's our policy.'" Sammy's response to this—"That's policy for you. Policy is what the kingpins want"—foreshadows that his decision to defy Lengel and "policy" will be signified by his baring his own shoulders, and that is precisely what occurs: "I pull the bow at the back of my apron and start shrugging it off my shoulders." The physical and emotional freedom which Sammy experiences by lifting off the symbolic yoke of the A & P uniform is quite palpable. He pulls off the constrictive bow tie (it's "theirs, if you've ever wondered"); and, relieved to be able to make "a clean exit, there's no fumbling around getting your coat and galoshes" in the summer-time, Sammy "just saunter[s] into the electric eye in my white shirt that my mother ironed the night before." The details of Sammy's departure suggest purity ("clean exit," "white shirt"), freedom ("just saunter"), and a sense of identity ("my white shirt," "my mother"—not "theirs") which had not been evident in the supermarket. It cannot be over-emphasized that people get dressed to enter the world of the A & P: "the women generally put on a shirt or shorts or something before they get out of the car." Further, that attire either constricts the body (Sammy says he literally felt his stomach "rub the inside" of his apron as he observed Queenie) or conceals its natural shape and color (Stokesie's pineapple-juice customer wears "baggy gray pants"). It is singularly appropriate, then, that rejecting the A & P (and the constrictive, artificial world which it represents) is symbolized by removing clothing—that is, by approximating the natural attire of the almost-naked girls. This clarifies why Updike did not make the girls especially pretty. The "chunky" one has "one of those chubby berry-faces, the lips all bunched together," while "Big Tall Goony-Goony" has "black hair that hadn't quite frizzed right, and one of those sunburns right across under the eyes, and a chin that was too long." Even Queenie has "a kind of prim face" and a neck that "looked kind of stretched." These are decidedly not what M. Gilbert Porter characterized as "three bathing beauties"; indeed, they don't even try to use make-up to conceal their flaws, unlike Sammy's nasty HiHo customer ("a witch about fifty with rouge on her cheekbones and no eyebrows"). · The girls' average appearance clarifies that Sammy, Lengel, and the customers are responding not to their looks, not even to their semi-nudity *per se*, but rather to the *naturalness* of their demeanor. The girls have more than just what Robert Detweiler terms "class": they have a willingness to act and look naturally in a world which does its best to contain or deny our natural impulses. Whether one sees Sammy as a would-be courtly lover, an Emersonian idealist, or a fool, the act of lifting the A & P apron from his shoulders shows that, at least for a while, he was indeed defying the artificial world of the A & P.

—Alice Hall Petry, "The Dress Code in Updike's 'A & P,'" *Notes on Contemporary Literature* 16, no. 1 (January 1986): pp. 9–10.

PATRICK W. SHAW ON THE SIMILARITIES BETWEEN "A & P" AND "YOUNG GOODMAN BROWN"

[Patrick W. Shaw, the author of *Literature: A College Anthology,* writes that Updike's narrative shares many similarities with the Nathaniel Hawthorne tale "Young Goodman Brown" (for example, the similar settings). In this extract, Shaw studies the use of the color pink in both texts to present the sexual connection that the color evokes. Shaw sees in both Sammy and Goodman Brown similar reactions rooted in Calvinist intolerance; these reactions render the protagonists helpless in the face of sexual stimuli.]

Updike also uses the emblematic value of pink dualistically in characterizing his young woman, as does Hawthorne. In "Young Goodman Brown," pink conveys the paradox of Faith's innocence (white) and the violence of her passions (red). Updike borrows from and extends this symbolism. Just as Faith's pink ribbon epitomizes innocence masking passion, Queenie's pink suit suggests the emerging desires competing with chastity. She is sincere and accurate when she tells Lengel that she is "decent," yet the protest is ironic. She may not consciously set out to entice males when she enters the A&P packaged in her revealing bathing suit, but her unconscious intent is quite another matter. Like all else in the store, her innocence seems for sale—something clearly implied by her casual lifting of the dollar bill from between her breasts.

Updike further uses pink as a clue to why Sammy responds as he does. Goodman Brown's paranoia comes in large measure from his ambiguous reaction to Faith's desires and his ultimate failure to reconcile his "evil" sexuality with his spiritual teachings. Because nothing in his catechisms has prepared him for Faith's sensuality, a life of guilt and remorse is his lot. Modern Sammy unknowingly echoes Goodman's dilemma when he describes Queenie's suit as being "dirty-pink"—dirty being a pejorative term connoting the puritan disapproval which taints Sammy's views and which helps us understand that Sammy's sudden quitting is not only a way of attracting the girls' attention but also a way of punishing himself for lustful thoughts. He periodically congratulates himself for having no sexual responses to the "houseslaves in pin curlers," with their varicose veins and dowdy attire. Queenie, however, allows him no such smugness. Conditioned by containers and packaging, Sammy is overpowered by the nubile body and its not-so-hidden persuasions. Queenie attracts him like a bee to honey, a trite but appropriate simile which Sammy himself introduces with the bee-in-jar remark.

Such sexual responses are an expected biological reaction; but along with his normal desire comes guilt, the "dirty" residue of sincere emotions. Beneath Sammy's hip talk and cool facade lies an inheritor of the same Calvinist intolerance that wrecks Goodman Brown. Like Goodman, Sammy can deal with the obvious witches, because in his unsophisticated ethic they are physically unappealing and therefore evoke no lust. He cannot, however, cope with the sexy and nimble girl who strolls into his domain and who is far more destructive than the witchy housewives he feels so self-righteous about rejecting.

—Patrick W. Shaw, "Checking Out Faith and Lust: Hawthorne's 'Young Goodman Brown' and Updike's 'A & P,'" *Studies in Short Fiction* 23, no. 3 (Summer 1986): pp. 322–23.

WALTER WELLS ON THE SIMILARITIES BETWEEN "A & P" AND "ARABY"

[In this excerpt, Walter Wells, author of *Tycoons and Locusts: Hollywood Fiction in the 1930s*, builds on the critical belief that Updike emulates James Joyce in many of his narratives. Wells sees similarities between Joyce's "Araby" and Updike's "A & P." Here he contrasts the two young protagonists to prove his thesis.]

Like "Araby," "A & P" is told after the fact by a young man now much the wiser, presumably, for his frustrating infatuation with a beautiful but inaccessible girl whose allure excites him into confusing his sexual impulses for those of honor and chivalry. The self-delusion in both cases leads quickly to an emotional fall.

At 19, Updike's protagonist, Sammy, is a good bit older than Joyce's—at the opposite end of adolescence, it would seem. While in Joyce's boy we readily believe such confusion between the gallant and profane, I think we needn't assume that Sammy is likewise unable to distinguish between the two quite normal impulses. His attraction to the girl in the aisle is certainly far more anatomically and less ambiguously expressed than that of Joyce's boy to Mangan's sister. But it is Beauty that confounds the issue. When human aesthetics come into play, when the object of a young man's carnal desire also gratifies him aesthetically, that is when the confusion arises. In Irish-Catholic Dublin of the 1890s, such youthful beauty not surprisingly invokes analogies between Mangan's sister and the Queen of Heaven (though the swinging of her body and "the soft rope of her hair toss[ing] from side to side," which captivate the boy, hint at something less spiritual than Madonna worship). And while beauty's benchmarks in Sammy's more secular midcentury America *are* more anatomical than spiritual, Updike does have Sammy call his young *femme fatale* "Queenie," and he does make her the center of a "trinity" of sorts, showing her two friends at one point "huddl[ing] against her for relief."

Once smitten, both young protagonists become distracted, agitated, disoriented. Joyce's turns impatient "with the serious work of life." His teacher accuses him of idling. His heart leaps, his thoughts wander, his body responds "like a harp" to the words and gestures of Mangan's sister, which run "like fingers . . . upon the wires." Similarly, Updike's young hero can't remember, from the moment he spots Queenie in the aisle, which items he has rung up on the cash register.

Even details in the two stories are similar, Updike clearly taking his cues from "Araby." Both boys are excited by specified *whiteness* about the girls—Joyce's boy by "the white curve of her neck" and "the white border of [her] petticoat" in the glow of Dublin lamplight, Sammy by the "long white prima-donna legs" and the white shoulders to which he refers repeatedly. "Could [there]," he wonders, "have been anything whiter than those shoulders[?]" Joyce's boy also observes a nimbus surrounding Mangan's sister, "her figure defined by the light from the half-opened door." True, Mangan's sister comports herself more humbly than her American counterpart. Queenie walks, heavy-heeled and head high, with the haughty pride of the affluent, secularized American upper middle class. But her enticing whiteness, in Updike's sly parody, is also given a luminous, halo-like quality: "around the top of the cloth," says Sammy of the bathing suit that "had slipped a little on her . . . there was this shining rim."

—Walter Wells, "John Updike's 'A & P': A Return Visit to Araby," *Studies in Short Fiction* 30, no. 2 (Spring 1993): pp. 128–29.

Plot Summary of
"Ace in the Hole"

This short tale forms part of the collection of stories in *The Same Door*, Updike's first published collection of short stories. "Ace in the Hole" originally appeared in the *New Yorker* on April 9, 1955.

As the story begins, Fred "Ace" Anderson desperately needs to hear some music to deflect his fearful thoughts. The tubes in the car radio take a few minutes to warm up, and while he waits Ace worries that his wife will be furious with him, but the first sounds of music immediately have the desired effect. Ace relaxes, grabs a cigarette, and lights it with a match without missing a beat of the song's rhythm. "He rolled down the window and snapped the match so it spun end over end into the gutter. 'Two points,' he said, and cocked the cigarette toward the roof of the car. . . . He was beginning to feel like himself, Ace Anderson, for the first time that whole day, a bad day."

Ace sings along contentedly as the radio plays "Blueberry Hill," so absorbed that he doesn't notice the teenager in the car next to him at the stoplight until the other driver mocks Ace's singing. At first Ace shrugs off the teenager's derision as something he might have done a few years earlier, but when the younger driver spits at Ace's car, Ace's reacts more harshly: "'Now isn't that pretty?' Ace said, keeping one eye on the light. 'You miserable wop. You are *mis*erable.' While the kid was trying to think of some smart comeback, the light changed. Ace dug out so hard he smelled burned rubber."

Ace feels better as he leaves the surprised teenager in his wake. He goes to his mother's house to pick up his baby daughter, instead of letting his wife do this as is her routine. When he arrives, Ace reveals to his mother (and the reader) the source of his troubled mood: his boss, Mr. Friedman, has fired him.

His mother offers her support: "Well, I don't dare think what Evey will say, but I, for one, thank God you had the brains to get out of it. I always said that job had no future to it—no future of any kind, Freddy." His mother goes on to say that Ace and the baby could always live with her if Evey makes trouble for him.

Ace half-listens to his mother while he watches a boy across the street dribble a basketball, throw it, and land it in the net. Meanwhile, his mother offers her opinion about her daughter-in-law: "Evey's a wonderful girl of her own kind. But I've always said, and your father agrees, Roman Catholics ought to marry among themselves."

When Ace objects to this line of conversation, his mother changes the subject by telling her son that he was mentioned in the newspaper that day. This diversion has no effect on Ace, who is still observing the young boy with the basketball.

Ace takes his daughter and heads for the car, but then he remembers that his basketball coach, Mr. Behn, used to encourage his players to walk. So Ace walks with his little daughter down the street. By the time he reaches his house a block away, he has lost interest in the baby and puts her in the crib with some toys.

He goes to the bathroom and becomes absorbed with fixing his hair in front of the mirror. "Finally, he mussed the hair in front enough for one little lock to droop over his forehead, like Alan Ladd. It made the temple seem lower than it was. Every day, his hairline looked higher. He had observed all around him how blond men went bald first. He remembered reading somewhere, though, that baldness shows virility."

Turning on the television to entertain his daughter, he gets a can of beer and turns his thoughts to how his wife will react to his bad news. He feels vexed with both his wife and his mother: "It was bad enough, his mother always crowding him. . . . He hoped Evey wouldn't say anything that couldn't be forgotten. What women didn't seem to realize was that there were things you knew but shouldn't say."

As he reflects, Ace drinks his beer and looks for the newspaper article mentioning his name. The story mentions his unbroken high-school basketball record, but he is angry because the newspaper refers to him as Fred Anderson and not Ace. He cannot calm himself. "He wasn't hungry; his stomach was tight. It used to be like that when he walked to the gymnasium alone in the dark before a game and could see the people from town, kids and parents, crowding in at the lighted doors. But once he was inside, the locker room would be bright and hot, and the other guys would be there, laughing and towel-slapping, and the tight feeling would leave. Now there were whole days when it didn't leave."

The second half of Updike's short narrative begins with Evey Anderson's arrival. Her mood is sour and sarcastic, but Ace is unsure if she knows yet about the loss of his job. Their exchange of questions and short retorts intensifies Ace's anxiety.

Evey leaves the room to change the baby, and when she returns, she seems calmer. Ace begins the story he has rehearsed, but Evey is not interested in his prepared excuses; she only wants to know the truth about what happened. Ace explains that at the car lot where he worked, Mr. Friedman asked him to move a car. In doing so, Ace crushed the fender of another parked car. Ace explains that nobody could have avoided the accident. Evey is not convinced.

> "...You could have looked."
> "There just wasn't the space. Friedman said stick it in; I stuck it in."
> "But you could have looked and moved the other cars to make more room."
> "I guess that would have been the smart thing."

The discussion becomes more tense and quarrelsome. When Evey tells Ace that she is "fed up," Ace counters by telling her she should seek the advice of a priest. Evey responds angrily: "If you think . . . if for one rotten moment you think, Mr. Fred, that the be-all and end-all of my life is you and your hot-shot stunts. . . ."

Ace interrupts by pointing out that the baby has picked up Evey's fallen ashtray and is using it as a hat. He contends that he can tell his daughter is a natural athlete by the way she uses her hands, but he laments that Bonnie's talent will be wasted. "She's a natural . . . and it won't do her any good because she's a girl. Baby, we got to have a boy." Ace then turns on the radio and repeats the word "Baby" to his wife.

> In the moment before the tubes warmed up, Evey had time to say, "Wise up, Freddy. What shall we do?" The radio came in on something slow: dinner music . . . "Shall we dance?" he asked his wife, bowing.

Ace, despite Evey's insistence that they talk things over, wants only to relax, to enjoy the "cocktail hour," and to think about having a son. "'Fred Junior. I can see him now,' he said, seeing nothing." Ignoring Evey's negative response, Ace puts his arm around his wife and leads her around the room to the rhythms of the music.

In the end, he is successful at distracting her, keeping up with the beat, swinging her to his tempo: "The music ate through his skin and mixed with the nerves and small veins; he seemed to be great again, and all the other kids were around them, in a ring, clapping time." ❀

List of Characters in
"Ace in the Hole"

Fred "Ace" Anderson is a young man, a former athletic star, who has fallen on bad times. He has lost his job and must admit this to his wife. Ace needs music to keep from worrying about his wife's reaction. When Ace is most stressed, he remembers his glory days as a record-setting basketball player.

Evey Anderson is Ace's young wife and the mother of his daughter; Evey is the responsible one in the family who does not tolerate Ace's thoughtless behavior. Through her sarcastic remarks, Evey reveals her disappointment in Ace and her concerns about their future.

Bonnie Anderson is Ace and Evey's daughter; the little toddler is cared for during the day by her grandmother. Bonnie's actions often divert the tense discussions of her parents. Ace believes that she has natural athletic abilities.

Mrs. Anderson is Ace's mother; she defends her son's actions and offers to let Ace and the baby live with her, speculating that since Evey is Catholic, her son might be better off on his own.

Mr. Friedman is the owner of the car lot. He fires Ace from his job when Ace backs into another car, damaging its fender. ✸

Critical Views on
"Ace in the Hole"

DONALD J. GREINER ON ACE'S CHARACTER

[Donald J. Greiner has published critical articles on James Dickey and Frederick Busch, as well as other essays on Updike's work. Here Greiner states that Ace Anderson foreshadows the principal character of *Rabbit, Run*. In Greiner's opinion, this short story is too limited for a complex reader response to Ace; instead, Greiner indicates that Updike exploits the "nuances of mood" in this story over the richness of dialogue found in the novel. Greiner further maintains that Ace remains a sympathetic character because of his refusal to quit in the face of hard luck and family criticism.]

The boy has grown up but has not made good in "Ace in the Hole." The germ of the later novel *Rabbit, Run*, this story also captures the details of the 1950s. "Blueberry Hill" is a hit tune, and "ducktails" are the male hairstyle of the day. Fred "Ace" Anderson foreshadows Harry "Rabbit" Angstrom, the small-town basketball hero who finds himself on the sidelines several years after graduation from high school. The future is nowhere in sight. All that exist are past memories and present motion. Only the rhythm of graceful movement sustains Ace. Worried about his situation, he picks a cigarette from the pack, moves it to his mouth, strikes a match, lights it, inhales, and blows out the flame all in time to "Blueberry Hill." But he is a one-time athlete now out of shape. One half-a-block sprint and two flights of stairs make him pant.

Unlike *Rabbit, Run*, the story does not give Updike the room to develop the potentially complex reader attitude divided between disapproval of Ace's longing to be a teen-aged star again and understanding of his instinct to enjoy life, to lash out at a dull domestic routine which cramps his easy motion and natural grace. Still, the story works well. Because it relies more on the nuances of mood than on the counterpoint of dialogue, "Ace in the Hole" is a better illustration of the developing Updike style than "Friends from Philadelphia." Ace can put a ball through the hoop, but he cannot park a used car in a lot. This time the crisis is real, something his usual show of indifference cannot shrug off. He is fired. His gradual loss of stature and hence identity is shown when the daily newspaper reviews his past scoring records but calls him Fred instead of Ace. He does not protest when Evey stuffs the sports page into the trash-can. In a few years he will reach the point that so terrifies Rabbit: "They've not forgotten him; worse, they never heard of him."

What makes Ace sympathetic is his refusal to give up. After a muted argument with his wife about being fired, he recovers a bit of his rhythm by jitterbugging with her. He daydreams about both past and future, about when he was a star and when his as yet unconceived son will inherit his athletic skills. He is one of Updike's earliest characters to experience what becomes a general dilemma: How to reconcile the need for freedom and applause with the demands of stability and family. Compromise seems impossible, for it suggests a fatal loss of momentum. Grabbing his wife for the dance, Ace does not so much jitterbug away his problem as keep himself in motion. The crisis will remain after the music stops, but for the moment he must dance within the freedom of the improvised pattern, keeping time with the only rhythm he is willing to acknowledge. Perhaps his son will inherit his sense of grace and coordination, and thus keep him alive, but behind that hope rests the dimly sensed fear that once his marriage becomes routine the dance band will call it a night:

> . . . he spun her out carefully, keeping the beat with his shoulders . . . he could feel her toes dig into the carpet. He flipped his own hair back from his eyes. The music ate through his skin and mixed with the nerves and small veins; he seemed to be great again, and all the other kids were around them, in a ring, clapping time.

Ace does not grow up because the realities of adult life which normally jolt people out of adolescence only make him retreat to the flickering spotlight of past glories and the dim echoes of applause. "Ace in the Hole" is not a typical initiation story because Ace neither learns nor is disillusioned. Despair may set in later as the result of early fame too easily won, but for the moment directionless momentum is all. Perhaps his mother is too indulgent and his wife too prosaic. Perhaps his job is dull and his capabilities limited. But none of this is to the point. Updike shows astonishing skill for one just beginning his career as a fiction writer. He convinces the reader to understand, sympathize with, and most of all regret the already wasted life of a young man in motion whose joy at fluid movement will join his inability to cope and lead him eventually into a cul-de-sac.

—Donald J. Greiner, *The Other John Updike* (Athens: Ohio University Press, 1981): pp. 67–68.

CLINTON S. BURHANS JR. ON THE SIMILARITIES OF ACE ANDERSON AND FLICK WEBB

[Clinton S. Burhans Jr., the author of critical essays on Crane and Hemingway, compares the "bypassed athletic hero" represented by Fred "Ace" Anderson in "Ace in the Hole" with the character of Flick Webb in a poem from Updike's *The Carpentered Hen*.]

In an early poem from *The Carpentered Hen*, "Ex-Basketball Player," Updike describes the once-great Flick Webb:

Once Flick played for the high-school team, the Wizards.
He was good: in fact, the best. In '46
He bucketed three hundred ninety points
A county record still. The ball loved Flick.
I saw him rack up thirty-eight or forty
In one home game. His hands were like wild birds.

He never learned a trade, he just sells gas,
Checks oil, and changes flats. Once in a while,
As a gag, he dribbles an inner tube,
But most of us remember anyway.
His hands are fine and nervous on the lug wrench.
It makes no difference to the lug wrench, though.

Off work, he hangs around Mae's luncheonette.
Grease-gray and kind of coiled, he plays pinball.
Smokes thin cigars, and nurses lemon phosphates.
Flick seldom says a word to Mae, just nods
Beyond her face toward bright applauding tiers
of Necco Wafers, Nibs, and Juju Beads.

Here, Updike simply presents a man alive only in his memories of a youthful glory. Apart from the stereotypical pathos of such a man, Flick Webb apparently has no particular significance for Updike.

In a short story, "Ace in the Hole," however, he complicates the problems of the bypassed athletic hero by extending it into personal and social relationships. A former basketball star and still holder of the county scoring record, Fred "Ace" Anderson has just been fired from another job. Driving home, he finds solace in snapping a match accurately into the gutter, like a basketball through a hoop, and by beating some boys in a race after stopping for a red light. He goes to his mother's to pick up his baby daughter, and his mother tells him to be glad he was fired—he was much too good for the job. At home, his wife, tired from working, is upset and wonders sarcastically what he plans to do now. Ace evades the issue by telling her that they must have a son to bring up as a basketball player and by making her dance with him. More and more, Ace feels "crowded" by his mother and by his wife and "tight," as he used to feel before a game. Then, the "tightness" vanished in the camaraderie of the locker room and in his feeling of greatness as a player; now, that feeling returns to him only in such trivial actions such as snapping matches and intersection drag racing and in the memories evoked by dancing: "he seemed to be great again, and all the other kids were around them, in a ring, clapping time."

Withdrawn and uninvolved with others, Flick Webb is apparently resigned to living in his memories of former glory. But Ace Anderson is more complex and significant, both in himself and in his relationships with others. More than just memories of past greatness, he wants something to recover that feeling in the present. His actions and reactions influence and are influenced by the many other people whose lives intersect with his; his mother, his wife, his daughter, the youths whom he understands and envies. Apart from the intrinsic pathos of his situation, then, Flick Webb has no meaning; but Ace Anderson, in his implied complexities and in the network of his relationships, offers a variety of human and sociological implication. An increasing imaginative grasp of these implications must have led Updike to see in Ace a point of view from which to study such a man and the culture which shaped him.

—Clinton S. Burhans Jr., "Things Falling Apart: Structure and Theme in *Rabbit, Run*," in *Critical Essays on John Updike*, William R. Macnaughton, ed. (Boston, Mass.: G. K. Hall and Co., 1982): pp. 152–53.

[The author and editor of books on modern fiction and a professor of Comparative Literature at Emory University, Robert Detweiler at first compares "Ace in the Hole" to *Rabbit, Run*. Detweiler goes on to point out the short story's "sheer verbal craftsmanship" revealed in the plot's tense and nervous movement. In this excerpt, Professor Detweiler also elucidates his interpretation of the double meaning of the story's title.]

Updike has, amazingly, already found his métier in "Ace in the Hole." The story offers less in terms of plot and action than "Friends from Philadelphia" but much more in terms of pure mood created out of sheer verbal craftsmanship. It is, much like *Rabbit, Run*, a sustained metaphor of nervous movement and a tension of opposites. Ace is always in motion: driving the car, smoking hastily, tapping a foot in rhythm, running home from his mother's house with the small daughter in his arms—still shifting restlessly on life's basketball court, trying to score and to be the hero again with the effortlessness of the natural. But Ace is not a natural in the workaday world. An indulgent mother and cheap early fame have spoiled him, and he is already a clearcut failure at the approaching prime of life. The antagonistic characters, his opposites, make his plight the more obvious. The prowling high school youths who insult him at the traffic light only show him (like the boys playing back-alley basketball at the start of *Rabbit, Run*) the reckless innocence that he has lost. His weary and dispirited wife, with her dogged common sense, makes him seem more of a loser.

Apart from a sexual innuendo, the title has a double sense. The protagonist is Ace "in the hole": jobless, unprepared to be a man, and threatened with a spouse nearly ready to leave him. But he also *has* his ace in the hole: his animal charm and his instincts that will help him to survive even if he ruins others in the process. The story is an inversion of the maturation pattern, for the events that should jolt the initiate into growing up at last only cause him to fight reality with a wasteful nervous energy. "Ace in the Hole" seems authentic because it fashions a modern American type, the teenage hero seduced by quick success into thinking that the adult world is easy to conquer but who soon suffers disillusion and the gradual degeneration into bumhood. Olinger can be too kind, the family-community can be too generous, when it offers its sons what they should strive a lifetime to deserve—and then permits grace to turn quickly into judgment. Updike has forced more news about one dead end along the American way of life into one brief story than many writers manage to report in a whole novel. It is no wonder that he returned to the theme and the place and expanded the microform into *Rabbit, Run.*

—Robert Detweiler, *John Updike* (Boston: Twayne Publishers, 1984): pp. 11–12.

ROBERT M. LUSCHER ON MUSIC AND BASKETBALL

[Like other critics, Robert M. Luscher calls Rabbit Angstrom to mind in relation to Ace Anderson. In this excerpt from his chapter entitled "Poised on the Threshold: *The Same Door*," Luscher considers two elements that frame Ace's problematic transition from youth to maturity: music and the basketball court. Ace depends on the radio to assuage his fears of his wife's expected criticism, while the court, once his area of dominance, now contrasts with his inability to "score" as an adult.]

A former basketball star who has just lost his job, Ace—now literally "in the hole"—is an early version of Rabbit Angstrom, the more fully developed protagonist of Updike's novelistic tetralogy, but the short story does not allow him much space to run. Ace would rather hide his head, ostrich-like, than face his wife Evey with the news of his unemployment. When the inevitable confrontation occurs, he is able to deflect her criticisms by turning on the radio and grabbing her to dance.

Updike frames the story with music, Ace's temporary means of escape. The opening line informs the reader that "Ace needed the radio, especially today"; like John Nordholm, he seeks something to make him feel "so sure inside" and galvanize the self-confidence that can raise him above the mundane world. Although this confidence manifests itself in a flippant, adolescent fashion, Ace is capable of (but not comfortable with) assuming a more mature role. As he waits for the radio to warm up, his remarks reveal both sides of his personality: first, using a youthful idiom, he proclaims, "Jesus. She'll pop her lid"; then, irked by his voice's thin and scratchy quality, he adds in a more resonant tone and formal idiom, "She'll murder me." More adept at alternating than reconciling his adolescent tendencies with his mature ones, Ace is pulled both ways, conscious that his youth is receding and the tensions of marital responsibility are overtaking him. Despite his escapist tendencies, he is mature enough to realize that some compromise is inevitable, even as he tries to postpone it.

For Ace, the basketball court, like Hemingway's bullring, provided an opportunity to exhibit grace under pressure; such glory can be recaptured only in scattered moments—winning the drag race, running home instead of driving—but not without repercussions. Although not much older than the two boys he races, they call him "Dad," suggesting a wider gulf than age difference alone creates. Ace empathizes with their emotional state—"young and mean and shy"—but later regrets his own meanness in calling one a "miserable wop." In running the short distance home from his parents' house, he follows his old coach's advice, but inadvertently rouses his infant daughter and thus provokes derisive remarks from Evey. Even the newspaper's mention of his former record remaining unbroken arouses mixed emotions because the article calls him by his given name instead of by his youthful nickname. When Evey later shoves the paper in the trash, he makes no protest. While Ace exhibits a cavalier attitude to Evey about losing his job, he counters his mother's indulgent sympathy with a more resigned consciousness about life's realities and a defense of his wife. Ace recognizes that his mother's indulgence has left him unprepared to deal with life's exigencies, but confronted with Evey's pragmatism and burdened by his own guilt, he can only respond with evasions, using music and his charm as his "ace in the hole" when all else fails. Committed to marriage, Ace will not flee, but domestic tension makes him feel crowded. No longer is he scoring baskets surrounded by cheering fans, staving off anxiety; now, during marital skirmishes, the "tight feeling" is more difficult to vanquish.

The story's symmetrical construction, signaled by the almost exact repetition of the words "In the moment before the tubes warmed up" preceding a dialogue marker, shows that Ace has come full circle. The story ends as it begins, with Ace in motion, though this time he is spinning rather than going forward. Both Ace and Evey know that their problems remain, but Evey's rationality is finally no match for her husband's evasiveness. As the radio's music surges from the speaker, Updike's prose tunes up as well: "The music ate through his skin and mixed with the nerves and small veins; he seemed to be great again, and all the other kids were around them, in a ring, clapping time." This vision is Ace's charmed circle, an "unexpected gift" of past vitality arresting the conflict of the present, but it moves him no closer to resolving his problems and crossing the threshold into maturity.

—Robert M. Luscher, *John Updike: A Study of the Short Fiction* (New York: Twayne Publishers, 1993): pp. 8–9.

THOMAS W. FORD ON UPDIKE'S USE OF PUNS

[In addition to this essay on Updike's short story, Thomas W. Ford has written on A. B. Guthrie Jr. and Ezra Pound. In this piece, Ford examines Updike's use of puns by explaining the various nuances of the expression "ace in the hole." Ford contends that Ace does "score" in the end. As seen in this excerpt, he bases this conclusion on the reference to stud poker.]

Updike's use of puns—words and images that carry multiple meanings, setting up different patterns of thought that operate simultaneously within those images—is his trademark, his most prominent stylistic feature. Perhaps nowhere is this feature more clearly evidenced than in his short story "Ace in the Hole."

Fred "Ace" Anderson, a former high school basketball star (who incidentally anticipates the character Harry "Rabbit" Angstrom in *Rabbit, Run*), faces a crisis. He has been fired from his job as a used car salesman after damaging a car while backing into a space that was too small. Trying to excuse his actions to his wife, Evey, he says: "Nobody could have gotten into that hole. Even if it had hair on it." The overt sexual image is one of a number of meanings carried in the title. He is, of course, in a hole financially since he has lost his job, and he is in a hole of embarrassment over the criticism that he fears from his wife. In his past glory days as a basketball star, he was always perfect in putting the ball in the hole of the basket. Floating on the surface of the images in the story are implied links and associations connecting athletics, sexual experience, music, dance, rhythm, motion, and games.

Although the various images intertwine and are interdependent, one of the meanings suggested by the title seems to be central and is, in a sense, the glue that holds the parts together. In the game of stud poker, the phrase "ace in the hole" refers to an ace dealt and kept face down until the hand is over. By extension, the phrase often refers to anything that can be used for winning that is kept in reserve until needed for a victory. Ace will use his "ace in the hole" near the end of the story to win a victory over his wife. The reader is prepared for that outcome by a series of images relating to card games, including stud poker, a game especially appropriate for Ace who, as a former basketball hero, was viewed as a "stud" by high school girls because of his athletic and presumably sexual prowess.

—Thomas W. Ford, "Updike's 'Ace in the Hole,'" *The Explicator* 52, no. 2 (Winter 1994): pp. 122–23.

Charlie Reilly on "Ace" as the Source for *Rabbit, Run*

[Charlie Reilly has interviewed several literary figures, including Joseph Heller and Kurt Vonnegut. In this short excerpt from Reilly's interview with John Updike, Reilly questions Updike on the source of *Rabbit, Run*, and Updike refers to "Ace in the Hole" as the precursor of the theme later developed in the novel. According to this interview, Ace's character evolved from Updike's curiosity about the figure of an athlete past his prime.]

Reilly: In 1957, you published a poem called "Ex-Basketball Player." Was that the source of *Rabbit, Run*?

Updike: The ultimate source is not particularly literary. Berks County, Pennsylvania, is crammed with ex-basketball players and, because my father was a ticket-taker, I went to a lot of games. My first treatment of the theme was a story I wrote in my senior year in college. It's called "Ace in the Hole" and, if you haven't seen it, it was re-printed in *The Same Door*. It's the oldest piece in there, even older than the title story. I wrote the poem, "Ex-Basketball Player," the first summer I was out of college, although it took about a year for *The New Yorker* to publish it. I have fond memories of the poem: it was one of the very first of my verses which *The New Yorker* published, and it's far and away my most anthologized poem. Indeed, that single poem has probably made more money than all my others put together. So, the theme for *Rabbit, Run* was simply there, and I wouldn't say the novel derived from the story or the poem as such. All of them came out of my interest in the phenomenon of an athlete outliving his time.

—Charlie Reilly, "A Conversation with John Updike," *Canto* 3, no. 3 (1980). Reprinted in *Conversations with John Updike*, James Plath, ed. (Jackson: University Press of Mississippi, 1994): p. 144.

Plot Summary of
"Flight"

This narrative, which first appeared in the New Yorker on August 22, 1959, is the fourth short story in *Pigeon Feathers and Other Stories*. It also makes up part of the collection *Olinger Stories*.

The young narrator, Allen Dow, reveals that at one point in his life he always spoke about himself in the third person. To provide some background as an explanation for this habit, Allen recounts an episode from when he was eleven or twelve. His mother walked with him up to the fashionable section of town known as Shale Hill, where they could view the better homes in the town of Olinger along with those one- and two-family houses more like the one in which Allen lived. From this encompassing view, his mother announced: "'There we all are, and there we'll all be forever.' She hesitated before the word 'forever,' and hesitated before adding, 'Except you, Allen. You're going to fly.'"

A flock of birds took flight as his mother spoke, but Allen was too embarrassed and irritated by her words to pay full attention to the birds. Quickly, his mother discarded her Cassandra-like vision by treating Allen once again as an ordinary child. Because of her change in attitude, Allen feels he was "captive to a hope she had tossed off and forgotten." He adopted the image of flight as his own, intending to exploit his mother's predictions. His identification with this image confused his relationship with his mother; she protested once: "You'll never learn, you'll stick and die in the dirt just like I'm doing. Why should you be better than your mother?"

His mother, Allen explains, was raised on a farm. Every Friday she rode to market on a wagon driven by Allen's grandmother. The wagon rides implanted a sense of fear in the small girl; she worried about breaking down, about being accosted by beer-drinking men, about coming home to a drunken father.

Allen's own recollection of his grandfather does not tally with this image, though. He remembers the man an avid reader of his Bible and the newspapers. His grandparents' life and luck on the farm had not been easy. But during a more prosperous time, his grandfather had enough money to invest in stocks and purchase a large home in town; Allen thinks that "The dignity of finance for the indignity of farming must have struck him as an eminently advantageous exchange."

These generational misunderstandings go even further back to Allen's great-grandfather, who was remembered by Allen's mother as "a saintly slender giant." However, his son, Allen's grandfather, remembers his father's sarcastic words best: "Pick up your feet; they'll come down by themselves." These thoughts of earlier paternal generations overshadow the little Allen recollects of his grandmother; he remembers only that she talked little, fed him too much, and died when Allen was seven.

His narration now turns again to his mother; he constructs an image of his mother from "one of the curling photographs kept in a shoebox that I was always opening as a child, as if it might contain the clue to the quarrels in my house." In this photo, Allen sees his mother as graceful, formidable, and well dressed. In contrast, Allen's father was a "penniless younger son of a Presbyterian minister" who worked his way through the same college where his mother studied. Allen returns to the clothing snobbery of his mother to comment on how she always bought his clothes at the best store in town, which meant, since there was little money, that he had few clothes but that they were expensive.

Returning to the photo, Allen explains that it was taken at a time when Allen's mother wanted to go to New York but that "her father forbade her," thus sowing the seeds for future heated accusations between daughter and father. Allen surmises that her disappointment and anger may have been the reason she married his father.

The couple moved away from the home of Allen's mother, so that Allen's father could start his career with an engineering firm. When the Depression hit and Allen's father lost his job, however, they moved back to the large house in town. The times were indeed difficult for the extended family: the grandfather witnessed the decline of his investments, the grandmother became a cleaning lady and sold produce grown in their yard, and the mother, after Allen's birth, worked in the fabric department in a nearby store. During Allen's first year, his father cared for him. "And that same shared year helps account, perhaps, for his gentleness with me, for his willingness to praise, as if everything I do has something sad and crippled in it. He feels sorry for me; my birth coincided with the birth of a great misery, a national misery. . . ."

In a gentler tone, different from the one he uses in his description of his mother, Allen relates that his father then got a job teaching mathematics in the local high school. Allen assumes that this position caused his kind and humorous father years of discomfort, but he acknowledges that the job also gave his father the opportunity to encourage and shape at least a few of his students.

During these trying years, Allen's grandfather was the last to join the work force—on a street-tarring crew. Ashamed and embarrassed, the grandfather refused to acknowledge Allen as he walked by the crew on his way to school. This work continued until the grandfather lost his sight; he then retired to a chair by the house's bay window. Allen was given the job of reading the newspapers to his grandfather.

Allen thought he could avenge his mother's past disappointments and grievances by reading too loudly or too quickly to his grandfather. Allen remarks, however, that "It would dawn on me then that his sins as a father were likely no worse than any father's. . . . But my mother's genius was to give the people closest to her mythic immensity. I was the phoenix. My father and grandmother were legendary invader-saints. . . ." This observation helps Allen come to a realization about his mother: "For my mother felt that she and her father alike had been destroyed by marriage, been made captive by people better yet less than they." Thus it is Allen's destiny, imposed by his mother's early prediction, to reverse this family fate.

Allen shifts the time of his narration from this chronicle of his family's past to events in his own life in his last year of high school. The school debate team, made up of Allen and three girls, boarded a train one Friday morning in October to travel to another school over one hundred miles away. Two of the girls, Judith and Catharine Miller, were known to Allen, but the third girl, Molly Bingaman, was a last minute substitute: "I knew her just by seeing her in the halls and in assembly. From a distance she seemed dumpy and prematurely adult. But up close she was gently fragrant, and against the weary purple cloth of the train seats her skin seemed luminous. She had beautiful skin, heartbreaking skin a pencil dot would have marred, and large blue eyes equally clear."

Their team won the Friday afternoon debate, the first of the weekend series. That night a dance was held in the gym of the high school to host the cycle of debates. Allen "conscientiously pushed Judith and Catharine around the floor" but spent most of the evening dancing with Molly. All four left the dance early and walked to the house where they were staying.

After Judith and Catharine went in, Allen and Molly remained outside, deciding instead to take a walk, which lasted until well past midnight. They stopped at a diner, ate, and returned to their hosts' home, where they stayed in the living room talking for several more hours. They ended their evening with their first tentative kiss.

The team lost the Saturday morning debate and the audience booed Allen's performance. On the train ride home Allen took solace in Molly's company and kisses. The parents met the team at the train station.

While Mr. Dow praised his son for the one debate they did win, Allen's mother attacked Molly and her family: "Why, when she stepped off the train from the way her chins bounced I thought she had eaten a canary. And then making my poor son, all skin and bones, carry her bag. When she walked by me I honestly was afraid she'd spit in my eye." At Allen's feeble defense of Molly, Mrs. Dow turned her remarks toward her husband to say: "You see, Victor—he defends her. When I was his age that girl's mother gave me a cut I'm still bleeding from, and my own son attacks me on behalf of her fat little daughter. . . ."

Soon, Allen noticed that his friends, some teachers, and even the luncheonette owner are against his relationship with Molly. He notes: "The entire town seemed ensnarled in my mother's myth, that escape was my proper fate." Molly's parents, on the other hand, did not object outwardly, but privately did not consider Allen to be socially acceptable.

His mother's feelings about her son's relationship with Molly were mixed up with her pain at attending to her dying father. Allen admits, "Every time I saw my mother cry, it seemed I had to make Molly cry. I developed a skill at it; it came naturally to an only child who had been surrounded all his life by adults ransacking each other for the truth."

As a consequence, Allen humiliates Molly even in their most private moments and avoids any open declaration of love. He compounds his confusion and grief by participating in too many school activities. On a particularly difficult night at home, while working on a yearbook entry, Allen suddenly leaves, takes the family car, and drives to Molly's house, only to park across the street to watch the house.

They had recently broken up, so Allen is surprised to see Molly in the front door with her coat on, as though she is ready to go out with him.

Her mother screams at her as Molly walks toward Allen's car. This becomes Allen's lasting memory of Molly: that she came to him.

Several hours later, when Allen finally returns home, his mother is waiting for him with a typically vulgar comment about Molly. Only his sick grandfather's singing interrupts their abusive discussion. Allen gives in to his mother's wishes. "In a dry tone of certainty and dislike—how hard my heart had become!—I told her, 'All right. You'll win this one, Mother; but it'll be the last one you'll win.'"

The statement leaves Allen on the edge of fulfilling his mother's prediction, bereft of senses until his mother's retort brings back his attention: "In a husky voice that seemed to come across a great distance my mother said, with typical melodrama, 'Goodbye, Allen.'" ✾

List of Characters in
"Flight"

Allen Dow is 17-year-old who struggles to understand his mother's early prediction that one day he will fly, meaning that he will escape from the destructive hold of ordinary life that binds her and Allen's extended family.

Lillian Dow is Allen's mother. As a young girl, her childhood growing up on a farm was marked by her tense and confrontational relationship with her father. Her bitterness colors her adult life and inspires her to look for a new and different future for her son Allen.

Victor Dow is Allen's sweet and humorous father; though trained to be an engineer, he teaches mathematics at the local high school. Allen's narration mentions his father less than his mother but with more tenderness and at times with a tone of pity.

Allen's grandfather is the elder member of the family, who represents both the harsh childhood Allen's mother endured and the financial difficulties that the family suffers as a result of the Depression.

Judith and Catharine Miller are two seniors from Allen's high school who, like Allen, travel to a debate competition as representatives of their school. They act somewhat as matchmakers for Allen and a fourth girl on the debate team.

Molly Bingaman is the fourth member of the debate team. Molly soon becomes an integral part of Allen's life and his struggle to understand and cope with his mother's seething need for him to leave. ❀

Critical Views on
"Flight"

[The Hamiltons have jointly written critical essays on Updike and Beckett. Here they lay the story "Flight" next to Updike's *Of the Farm* to compare the boys in each narrative, their relationships with their mothers, and their choices of girls despite strong maternal objections. Joey, in *Of the Farm*, rejects his mother's wishes to become a poet, while Allen, in "Flight," eventually gives into his mother's prediction of escape.]

The relationship between Joey and his mother finds its point of greatest tension in her desire for a country life which made her insist—against the wishes of husband, father, and son—on bringing the family to the farm. Her love of Nature, emphasized in "Pigeon Feathers" and in *The Centaur*, is not the instinctive love of working on the land which characterized her own mother, but is one with her love of Greek. It is a platonic love (Nature with a capital "N"), as *Of the Farm* makes clear; for the practically-minded Richard asks at the beginning of the book, "What's the point of having a farm nobody farms?" In this regard, it is one with her love of Art and her dislike of the bourgeois standards represented, in her eyes, by Olinger. Joey, like Peter and like George (in both books), cannot understand this love; but he does come to see something of its positive worth.

The story which stands in the closest relation to *Of the Farm* is "Flight," in *Pigeon Feathers*. This short story is about Allen Dow's love for the Olinger girl Molly Bingaman when he was seventeen, and about his mother's strenuous opposition to the association of her son with this "stupid" girl. (Mrs. Robinson insists that Peggy is a stupid woman; and Joey, like the boy Allen, cannot deny this.) Allen, dismayed by his mother's fury and by the general disapproval he finds around him of his chosen love, first torments Molly and makes her cry, and at last breaks with her when he finds she comes to him too easily. They never reach the point of sexual intercourse, but Allen discovers from her—and this is the reason for his joy in her—that a man can "bury a humiliation in the body of a woman."

"Flight" is so called because Allen's mother fancies that her son, through his artistic talent, is going to fly like a bird beyond the mean limits of Olinger. In this story the platonic vision of Lillian Dow fuses with Allen's discovery of romantic love. Allen is his mother's son in refusing Molly Bingaman when the ideal image threatens to become a limited reality. *Of the Farm* repeats the same pattern. Joey cannot share his mother's love of the beauty and peace seen on the face of nature, but he does respond to her wish for him to be a poet. Like his father, he is a city boy at heart, and at this point he asserts his independence and goes to make a career for himself in New York. But he marries Joan because she is a poetic image belonging to the world his mother wishes for him. When he first met her, he says, "she suggested, remote and lithe and inward, the girl of 'The Solitary Reaper' and, close-up, seemed a cool Lucy whose death might give me cause to sing." However, marriage with the remote, inward, and cool woman of romantic poetry proved a disappointment. A platonic ideal is ill-suited to the intimacies of bed and board. And, having decided not to be a singer, Joey turns from his Wordsworthian fancy for the far-away-and-long-ago and discovers another woman in whose body he can forget his humiliation.

—Alice and Kenneth Hamilton, *The Elements of John Updike* (Grand Rapids, Mich.: William B. Eerdmans, 1970): pp. 186–87.

DONALD J. GREINER ON AMBIGUITY IN THE STORY

[Donald J. Greiner, the author of studies on James Dickey and Frederick Busch, points out in this excerpt the ambiguity of Allen's status in "Flight": the boy is both special and ordinary in his mother's eyes. Mrs. Dow marks his childhood with her prediction, and she shapes his future by her objections to his romantic relationship with Molly because it might keep her son tied to her town and her own hopeless life.]

Charles Thomas Samuels calls "Flight" perhaps the "most brilliantly written of the autobiographical tales," and I certainly agree. Although it is the first story in the collection told in the first person, "Flight" is a companion piece with "The Persistence of Desire" and "A Sense of

Shelter." Updike is especially good in suggesting the dual perspective of the boy going through the unsettling competition with his mother and of the mature man looking back on the experience. Not only does Allen Dow recall the time when he speaks of himself in the third person, he also remembers that the struggle with Mother has been going on for years. "Years before, when I was eleven or twelve, just on the brink of ceasing to be a little boy, my mother and I. . . ." From the vantage point of maturity, he now realizes that at age seventeen he was poorly dressed, funny-looking, and conscious that "a special destiny made me both arrogant and shy."

His sense of being special is ambiguous. Partly the result of Mrs. Dow's own frustration with her drab life, Allen's supposed specialness is also her most important dream for herself and her son. If we accuse her of trying to live through Allen, we must also recognize that her aspirations for his escape from the small town of Olinger save him from a similar frustration. "Flight" is the story of a mother-son relationship at a time in the boy's life when the father seems busy or asleep. Mrs. Dow prefigures the complex Mrs. Robinson in *Of the Farm* just as Mr. Dow becomes the Centaur. "Impulsive and romantic and inconsistent," the mother grudgingly accepts her static life in Olinger only because she is convinced that her son is going to "fly." But getting him into flight is her problem and his despair. She tells him at age twelve that he is special, and he thus becomes "captive to a hope she had tossed off and forgotten." Since she fears his "wish to be ordinary," she protests when he tries to fly the nest with Molly Bingaman without abandoning the limits of Olinger. This point is crucial to the story. Mrs. Dow is not so much against Molly as she is fearful that Molly will tie Allen to his hometown.

Updike is especially perceptive in capturing the uneasy ambivalence of Allen's predicament. He sketches in the sense of generations by describing in a few paragraphs the tensions that identify Allen's ancestors as far back as his great-grandfather. "Perhaps," says the mature Allen, "prolonged fear is a ground of love." Wondering if "each generation of parents commits atrocities against their children," he uses the memory of his adolescent love of Molly to ponder his relationship with his mother. The genius of "Flight" is that Allen's recollection of Mrs. Dow is as inconsistent as he claims she is. His descriptions hit the mark: She is precocious yet believes in ghosts; handsome, she has a deprecating smile; a fabric snob with a generous clothes allowance, she marries the penniless son of a minister; and though she obeys her own father, she, like Allen, tries to escape Olinger. The key to the relationship between Allen and his mother may be found in the mature Allen's realization that he has misunderstood her attitude toward her own father all along, that she fights with him not because of desperation or anger but because she cannot leave him alone. The same is true in the mutual relationship between mother and son. Allen needs to tell this story in order to understand a past which continues to puzzle him. Without the past, of course, there is no meaningful present and thus no basis for growth and knowledge. Allen's story is paradoxically both his most strenuous flight from and his most determined effort to know his roots. Plunging into the past in order to tell his tale, he hopes to soar from memory toward the future. He realizes now that he has successfully found his role in his mother's dreams for him, for Mrs. Dow is above all a mythmaker, a frustrated woman who gives those closest to her "mythic immensity." Allen is her phoenix. Believing that she and her father have been destroyed by marriage, she raises her son as a hero who will fly from the desolation of her domestic life and thereby redeem her.

No wonder she discourages his attraction to teen-aged girl friends. The second half of "Flight" details Allen's journey with three girls during his senior year in high school to debate at another school over one hundred miles from Olinger. There, away from mother and the inhibiting routine of home, Allen discovers the "beautiful skin, heartbreaking skin" of Molly to whom he has before not paid the slightest attention. He mistakenly thinks she frees him. He jokes with Molly, dances with Molly, and for the first time in his life stays up past midnight talking with Molly. From today's perspective, he has forgotten the details of what must have been a pivotal night in his adolescence: "What did we say? I talked about myself." Yet the experience lodges in his memory, and we suspect that his attraction to Molly has itself become mythologized in his mind as the first serious step away from mother.

How wrong he is at the time. Mrs. Dow sees the ostensible outward-bound footprint for what it is, a step toward married life in Olinger. Still clinging to the dream that her son will somehow soar from the small town and thereby atone for her own disappointing life, she counterattacks as soon as Allen returns from the trip: "Don't go with little women, Allen. It puts you too close to the ground." Unfortunately for the teen-ager, but luckily for the man, friends, teachers, and both sets of parents conspire to separate him from Molly: "The entire town seemed ensnarled in my mother's myth, that escape was my proper fate. It was as if I were a sport that the ghostly elders of Olinger had segregated from the rest of the livestock and agreed to donate in time to the air." His youthful vanity, as he now remembers, is so great that he believes all of Olinger focuses upon his plight. In his bewilderment, Allen criticizes Molly because the affair makes him see an "ignoble, hysterical, brutal aspect" of his mother. But things are not that simple. He recognizes now, although he fails to do so as a teen-ager, that Mrs. Dow's apparent pettiness results as much from the daily presence of her dying father as from her desire for Allen's flight. The competing tensions from two generations of men nearly exhaust her.

—Donald J. Greiner, *The Other John Updike* (Athens: Ohio University Press, 1981): pp. 103–5.

Mary Allen on the Manipulative Mother

[As Mary Allen points out, in "Flight" Updike distinguishes between the mother to be feared and the girl/wife/love interest to be embraced. Mrs. Dow's desire for excellence cannot be satisfied in her own life, so she projects this desire onto her son. In doing so, her needs are always selfish, in sharp contrast to Molly's need for Allen Dow. Allen argues against a wife-whore division in Updike's stories because of the presence of such manipulative mothers.]

Perhaps Updike's horror of the powerful, manipulative mother turns him with an extra fondness to the docile woman who can be dominated (and slept with). Most of his women characters belong to one of these two opposing types, each deadly in its way. Some readers see in Updike's women instead a wife-whore division, but the wife and whore often resemble each other, wives acting the part of whores and whores who are considered as possible wives. The mature mother, however, exerting much the same influence as the dominant figures of Kesey and Roth, is an overpowering presence in contrast to the pliable wives and lovers. The difference for Updike's men is that they are much more successful at escaping the mother than are the inmates of the Big Nurse and the son of Mrs. Portnoy. The oedipal problem—a mother is someone you cannot sleep with—for Updike seems to open the field to all others, a wide and delicious playground for his men. Hardly a woman here is without sexual appeal. And everything can be forgiven except frigidity.

The story "Flight" clearly distinguishes between mother, who is to be feared, and girl (or wife), who is to be embraced. When Allen Dow was eleven or twelve his mother climbed with him to the top of a hill, dug her fingers into his hair, and announced that he was going to fly away from the small town below them where everyone else would stay forever. Her genius is "to give the people closest to her mythic immensity," and her boy is to be a phoenix. When Allen takes a liking to the plump, kindly Molly Bingaman, Mrs. Dow hysterically resists this hindrance to his flight, proclaiming that to go with a little woman (she might as well have said any woman) "puts you too close to the ground." Mrs. Dow's vulgar reference to "little hotpants" as part of her general attempt to denigrate sexual love for Allen, however, is a failure. He now knows, after being booed at a debate and using Molly's shoulder for comfort, the marvelous possibility of burying a "humiliation in the body of a woman," which is so revered by Updike's men. A woman's body may also be used for celebration. After winning a basketball game, Rabbit Angstrom makes love. When other skills are gone, the act of love is often the only means left by which to prove a victory.

The portrait of Mrs. Dow as the archetypal manipulative mother is complicated by her genuine desire for excellence, which, having no outlet in her own life, is channeled through Allen. Fortunately, since Mrs. Dow's dream is for the boy's flight, she allows Allen to escape. Giving up Molly, he admits defeat to his mother but is determined he shall never do so again. Updike's young men usually learn quite early in their lives the necessity of getting away from mother, both literally and, as best they can, emotionally. They do not generalize the fear of her into a fear of all women and find most others to be kind and comforting by comparison.

The women in "Flight" recall the account of the author's own life in "The Dogwood Tree: A Boyhood" when young John's mother forbids him to kiss his girlfriend, which only increases his desire to do so. The fondness of this boy—"My love for that girl carries through all those elementary-school cloakrooms"—is reflected in the creation of nearly all of Updike's male characters. What the young Allen Dow appreciates most about Molly is that she returns his love. She even comes running to him with her mother yelling at her to turn back. The Updike male is utterly vulnerable to such a woman's need for him, a dependence that is seen as unselfish and desirable. By contrast, the mother's need is always selfish. Mrs. Dow is indicted by omission as Allen reminisces that Molly "seems the one person who loved me without advantage."

—Mary Allen, "John Updike's Love of 'Dull Bovine Beauty'" in *The Necessary Blankness: Women in Major American Fiction of the Sixties* (Urbana: University of Illinois Press, 1976). Reprinted in *John Updike*, Harold Bloom, ed. (New York: Chelsea House Publishers, 1987): pp. 69–70.

JAY CANTOR ON HYPERBOLE IN THE STORY

[In this extract, Jay Cantor, author of *The Space Between: Literature and Politics* as well as works of fiction, argues that Allen Dow's penchant for hyperbole compensates for the dullness of his reality. Cantor further states that Allen shares this talent with his mother, who predicts his special future only to focus on his ordinary present. Allen's love interest, Molly, does not demand this special status from him. The fascination of that which is special and not ordinary enslaves Allen to his mother's vision.]

Allen's gift for flight most definitely includes his own talent for hyperbole, a way of *making things interesting*. For as all writers know, actualities fall short. We require the glow that transference gives in our loves, and the spice of myth in our stories. But the writer must learn the technique of hyperbole, not drug himself with it, for a novel that is all hyperbole—like the work of Anaïs Nin, say—is, in this secular age, unconvincing, too unironic. Human gods are, after all, unreliable as sources of chosenness. Allen's mother is "impulsive and romantic and inconsistent. I was never able to develop this spurt of reassurance into a steady theme between us. . . . 'You'll never learn, you'll stick and die in the dirt just like I'm doing. Why should you be better than your mother?'" For a parent often wants a child to fly beyond her, but hates it when he seems about to leave her earthbound, aging, mortal. So the young aviator feels worthless if he fails, and grieves if he succeeds. Perhaps this accounts for the melancholy that haunts those who have gone beyond their parents, the sadness of immigrants and their children, of progress, of America.

Allen must redeem all that his implacable mother has suffered, "the inheritance of frustration and folly that had descended from my grandfather to my mother to me . . . that I, with a few beats of my grown wings, was destined to reverse and redeem." If he does not, she will withdraw his special fate—a chosenness that also allows him, barely, to withstand the black mass of suffering, the family history that she has transmitted, and that he must redeem. The power to realize his ambition and the necessity for it both come from his mother.

In "Flight," Allen fails his mother by loving a high-school girl that she finds ordinary. "Don't go with little women, Allen. It puts you too close to the ground." Allen, too, disparages Molly even as he describes her. "Except for a double chin, and a mouth too large and thick, she would have been perfectly pretty in a little woman's compact and cocky way." Yet when he is with her, Allen can be a self rather than strut the one that, like an ill-fitting suit, has been given him by another. With Molly, he doesn't have to think of himself in the third person; she does not require that he be a messiah. "We never made love in the final, coital sense," but "she gave herself to me anyway, and I had her anyway, and have her still, for the longer I travel in a direction I could not have taken with her, the more clearly she seems the one person who loved me without advantage. I was a homely, comically ambitious hillbilly. . . ."

Which woman—which sense of himself—shall he choose? He vacillates. "Every time I saw my mother cry, it seemed I had to make Molly cry. . . . Even in the heart of intimacy, half-naked each of us, I would say something to humiliate her. . . ." But there can be no real contest. He needs his mother's mythologizing to certify that he is special, and so protect him from that equally strong voice that says he is nothing, that he will stick in the dirt. Requiring her hyperbole as a drug against her sadness, he is a slave to her. Enslaved, how can he not be enraged by the feminine, and—as he so often does—denigrate it?

—Jay Cantor, "On Giving Birth to One's Own Mother," *TriQuarterly* 75 (Spring/Summer 1989): pp. 88–89.

[In his chapter called "Ceremonies of Farewell: *Pigeon
Feathers*," Robert M. Luscher, author of several essays on
Salinger and Dickinson, introduces his comments about
"Flight," referring to the story as "the volume's first retrospec-
tive first-person narration." Here Luscher compares "Flight" to
another Updike short story, "Still Life," and concludes that
"Flight" is the stronger story because of the interplay of ideas
that impels the plot.]

The title of "Still Life" serves as a clever metaphor for the lack of
progress in a romance between two art students of different nationali-
ties, yet it might also characterize the problems with this story: like his
protagonists, Updike has assembled all the elements for his composition, but they never quite cohere. Many of Updike's stories, in which
perception rather than action assumes primary importance, could be
likened to still lifes, but this tale finally lacks the pressure of memory,
the more dynamic tensions of domestic life, and the interplay of ideas
that impel Updike's better stories, such as "Flight," the volume's first
retrospective first-person narration, in which Allen Dow reexamines a
crucial emotional separation from Olinger—his mother in particular—
as he struggles to understand the burdens of the past. Mrs. Dow resem-
bles a refined and stronger version of *Winesburg, Ohio*'s Elizabeth
Willard, Sherwood Anderson's repressed and dreaming mother figure
who hopes to have her son enact the escape from the village that she
was unable to accomplish. Allen's mother, with her flair for the dra-
matic, creates the self-fulfilling prophecy of her son's flight, a com-
munal myth that he simultaneously rebels against and strives to make
his own while he inhabits the middle ground between the ordinary life
of Olinger to which he is attracted and her persistent vision of tran-
scendence. She nurtures his dream and stifles his rebellion so that he
will, like a phoenix rising from the ashes of her past, redeem her failure.

Allen resists his special destiny because he perceives that in leaving
Olinger, he will merely fulfill the expectations of the very community
he wishes to defy. Simultaneously flattered and rejected by the town, he
feels trapped in everyone else's dream, as if he "were a sport that the
ghostly elders of Olinger had segregated from the rest of the livestock
and agreed to donate in time to the air." Paradoxically, in her attempt to

steer him to freedom, his mother must restrict his options; in contrast, Allen's courtship of Molly Bingaman represents his attempt to shape his own destiny. While an oedipal reading of the conflict between Allen and his mother is certainly possible, Mrs. Dow's bitter hostility toward Molly arises from her fear that such an Olinger-bred "little woman" will keep Allen close to the ground; despite her personal barbs and the grudge she harbors from Mrs. Bingaman's past snub, Mrs. Dow fights not so much against Molly as against what she represents. Ironically, in her desire to see Allen soar beyond Olinger, she assumes a domineering, dictatorial role similar to one her father took when he forbade her to leave Olinger for New York. Yet Allen cannot typecast his mother as a villain in this story. In retrospect, he must face the unpleasant truth about his past behavior: he too has emotionally abused Molly, who, caught in the middle of their struggle, nonetheless returns unconditional love.

In striving to understand his mother, Allen seeks the sources of his present self; in the process, he touches her suffering and sacrifice, as well as the ambivalence of her relationship with her father. Updike singles out Allen's epiphany as an exceptional moment of insight: "chafing to escape . . . and a bit more of a man but not quite enough," Allen becomes attuned not only to his own feelings but also to the dreams of his mother and grandfather. "There has never been anything in my life quite as compressed, simultaneously as communicative to me of my own power and worth and of the irremediable grief in just living, in just going on" [Updike, interview with Charles Thomas Samuels]. Though Allen is casting off from his mother, she has indeed won the crucial battle, forcing him to be independent of both her and Molly: "the chair ceased to be felt under me, and the walls and furniture of the room fell away." As the supports of Olinger vanish from beneath his feet, he begins the flight away from boyhood. In his sensitized state, Allen reaches a rare comprehension of the ambivalent life beyond Olinger, of "the suppressed pain, with the amount of sacrifice I suppose that middle-class life demands" [Updike, interview with Charles Thomas Samuels]. Such insight, not the mere physical departure from Olinger, is perhaps the true flight he achieves in the story.

Beyond the confines of his native Olinger, Allen is nevertheless bound to his origins. Telling the story does not free him from the past; paradoxically, his narrative flight there and back only strengthens the ambivalent connection and highlights his loss. The mature Allen who narrates the story has progressed beyond the self-conscious and conceited adolescent who speaks of himself in the third person, as if his life were a novel in the making. Examining his former self across the distance of years rather than minutes, he discovers, proves to be a more complex operation, "just as it might be hard for a movie projector, given life, to see the shadows its eye of light is casting." Thus, in order to understand himself, he replays the lives of preceding generations, and discovers in their struggles the source of his own ambivalent love and the meaning of his flight.

—Robert M. Luscher, John Updike: A Study of the Short Fiction (New York: Twayne Publishers, 1993): pp. 26–28.

JOHN UPDIKE ON THE IMAGES OF ESCAPE AND LOSS IN THE STORY

[Charles Thomas Samuels has published critical essays on F. Scott Fitzgerald and Edgar Allen Poe, in addition to this article on John Updike. This excerpt comes from an interview he did with John Updike in 1967 on Martha's Vineyard. Here Updike denies any autobiographical importance in his writing, but he points to the "image of flight or escape or loss" present in *Pigeon Feathers and Other Stories* and especially in "Flight."]

Updike: In other words, I disavow any essential connection between my life and whatever I write. I think it's a morbid and inappropriate area of concern, though natural enough—a lot of morbid concerns are natural. But the work, the words on the paper, must stand apart from our living presences; we sit down at the desk and become nothing but the excuse for these husks we cast off. But aside from the somewhat teasing little connections, there is in these three novels and the short stories of *Pigeon Feathers* a central image of flight or escape or loss, the way we flee from the past, a sense of guilt which I tried to express in the story, the triptych with the long title, "The Blessed Man of Boston, My Grandmother's Thimble, and Fanning Island," wherein the narrator becomes a Polynesian pushing off into a void. The sense that in time as well as space we leave people as if by volition and thereby incur guilt and thereby owe them, the dead, the forsaken, at least the homage of rendering them. The trauma or message that I acquired in Olinger had to do with suppressed pain, with the amount of sacrifice I suppose that middle-class life demands, and by that I guess I mean civilized life. The father, whatever his name, is sacrificing freedom of motion, and the mother is sacrificing in a way—oh, sexual richness, I guess; they're all stuck, and when I think back over these stories (and you know, they *are* dear to me, and if I had to give anybody one book of me it would be the Vintage *Olinger Stories*), I think especially of that moment in "Flight" when the boy, chafing to escape, fresh from his encounter with Molly Bingaman and a bit more of a man but not enough quite, finds the mother lying there buried in her own peculiar messages from far away, the New Orleans jazz, and then the grandfather's voice comes tumbling down the stairs singing, "There is a happy land far far away." This is the way it was, is. There has never been anything in my life quite as compressed, simultaneously as communicative to me of my own power and worth and of the irremediable grief in just living, in just going on.

I really don't think I'm alone among writers in caring about what they experienced in the first eighteen years of their life. Hemingway cherished the Michigan stories out of proportion, I would think, to their merit. Look at Twain. Look at Joyce. Nothing that happens to us after twenty is as free from self-consciousness because by then we have the vocation to write. Writers' lives break into two halves. At the point where you get your writerly vocation you diminish your receptivity to experience. Being able to write becomes a kind of shield, a way of hiding, a way of too instantly transforming pain into honey—whereas when you're young, you're so impotent you cannot help but strive and observe and feel.

—Charles Thomas Samuels, "The Art of Fiction XLIII: John Updike," *Paris Review* 45 (Winter 1968). Reprinted in *Conversations with John Updike*, James Plath, ed. (Jackson, Miss.: University Press of Mississippi, 1994): pp. 27–29.

Plot Summary of
"Pigeon Feathers"

The title story from *Pigeon Feathers and Other Stories* was first published in the *New Yorker* on August 19, 1961. The story also was reprinted as part of the *Olinger Stories* collection.

The narrator explains that as a consequence of his family's move to Firetown from Olinger, David Kern's life has changed its tenor in subtle yet definitive ways. The old comfortable sofa where David spent afternoons "reading mystery novels and science fiction and P. G. Wodehouse" now stands in the barn covered by a tarpaulin. The blue wing chair once tucked away in a forbidding guest room now sits in front of a tiny fireplace, the only source of heat in the house. To compensate for his sense of displacement, David spends one Saturday trying to arrange the books.

This self-imposed task only serves to emphasize the changes in David's life, since even his choice of reading material has been affected by the move. He chooses now the Bible and H. G. Wells's *The Outline of History*, because he thinks these books will give him some sense of the gap in time between himself and his parents. Instead, however, David is provoked by Wells's account of Jesus: "He had been an obscure political agitator, a kind of hobo, in a minor colony of the Roman Empire. By an accident impossible to reconstruct, he (the small *h* horrified David) survived his own crucifixion and presumably died a few weeks later."

David is incredulous at such statements; he is certain they are falsehoods. In his mind, he reviews the evidence against Wells's account: churches standing all over the world, a nation founded "under God." How could "a black brain" like Wells's have been permitted to exist? David has to acknowledge, though, his own ignorance and lack of first-hand experience in regard to God's existence. After reviewing his childhood memories, his only consolation is to recall that his prayers have in fact been answered.

When his father returns home that Saturday, the ever-present arguments between his parents irritate David. His city-raised father maintains that everything concerning the earth is chemical in nature; David's mother, however, insists that the "land has a *soul*."

His grandmother, whose hands are crippled by Parkinson's disease, is an unwilling participant in their arguments. Quoting the Bible as his authority, George Kern insists that only humans have souls; then, turning to David, he delivers his opinion on women in general: "When God made your mother, He made a real femme."

Elsie Kern, agitated both by her husband's declaration and her mother's infirmity, yells in frustration at the older woman. "It was horrible but the horror was particular and familiar, and distracted David from the formless dread that worked, sticky and sore, within him, like a too large wound trying to heal."

David leaves and goes to the outhouse to relieve himself, despite his fear of the spiders inside the small shack. Inside the outhouse, he envisions an image of death: ". . . a long hole in the ground, no wider than your body, down which you are drawn while the white faces above recede. You try to reach them but your arms are pinned. Shovels pour dirt into your face. There you will be forever, in an upright position, blind and silent, and in time no one will remember you, and you will never be called."

An overwhelming sense of fear makes David break into a sweat. In the open air again, his terror begins to subside as he runs through the grass toward the house. But images out of science fiction—"the dilation of the sun, the triumph of the insects, the crabs on the shore in *The Time Machine*"—run after him.

Inside, the scene is calmer, but his parents continue on with a discussion of crops, chemicals, and earthworms. While his father likens his wife's beliefs to those of the Dark Ages, David consults the entry for soul in the copy of *Webster's Dictionary* that once belonged to his grandfather. The key phrase for David reads: "separate in nature from the body and usually held to be separable in existence."

His parents' relentless argument is peppered by his mother's silences that resonate with her anger. During a sudden outburst from his wife, Mr. Kern unexpectedly diverts the tension: "'Let's all go to bed,' David's father said, rising from the blue wing chair and slapping his thigh with a newspaper. 'This reminds me of death.' It was a phrase of his that David had heard so often he never considered its sense."

Once in bed, the clean, pressed sheets distract David from his fears. But his thoughts return to images of his own dying. David prays and lifts his hands high in the air, begging Christ to come down and touch him. Then he tucks his hands under the blankets, surmising that Christ's touch would be too gentle to notice.

The next morning, instead of accompanying his father to Sunday services, he walks out into the field with his mother. When she asks why he is troubled, David easily lies and denies that anything is troubling him. When they return to the house, they find that David's father had already come home. His father immediately returns to the debate with David's mother, contending that the minister was wasting his time preaching to the farmers, implying that all of them, including his father-in-law, were less than intelligent.

David occupies himself with the Sunday paper but has to leave his reading to attend the children's Sunday school session. David thinks of the girls in these gatherings as "dull white cows" and the boys as "narrow-faced brown goats in old men's suits." The catechism class normally embarrasses David, but this Sunday it holds out to him a sense of hope, for David is desperately seeking some gesture or sign that will comfort him.

Although David generally liked and appreciated the new minister, Reverend Dobson, at this Sunday school meeting, David finds no comfort or support in Dobson's evasive answers to David's question: "About the Resurrection of the Body—are we conscious between the time when we die and the Day of Judgment?" The best answer Dobson can come up with is that that souls are asleep during this time. The other children nervously giggle as the uncomfortable exchange between David and the minister continues: "'David, you might think of Heaven this way: as the way the goodness Abraham Lincoln did lives after him.'

"'But is Lincoln conscious of it living on?' He blushed no longer with embarrassment but in anger; he had walked here in good faith and was being made a fool."

David feels Dobson's answers to be fraudulent, but his anger at Dobson shifts to shame. As he returns home, he feels hardened by this betrayal of Christianity's essence by a minister, one of its own.

Once home, David consults his grandfather's Bible. When his mother notices this, she again asks what is troubling her son. As they discuss Reverend Dobson and David's disappointment in his answers, Mrs. Kern tries to shift her son's attention to the beautiful April day as proof of God's existence. David responds:

> "He made everything. You feel that?"
> "Yes."
> "Then who made Him?"
> "Why, Man. Man." The happiness of this answer lit up her face radiantly, until she saw his gesture of disgust. She was so simple, so illogical; such a femme.

Like his father, David dismisses the validity of her argument, but as she persists, the effect of her words on David change: ". . . all her grace, her gentleness, her love of beauty, gathered into a passive intensity that made him intensely hate her."

He escapes outside, but when he comes back in the house, his mother gives him her college text of Plato and suggests he read the "Parable of the Cave." David tries to shake off his mother's attentions. Sensing this, Mrs. Kern announces to her husband that their son is worried about death. His father responds: "Don't give it a thought, David. I'll be lucky if I live till tomorrow, and I'm not worried. If they'd taken a buckshot gun and shot me in the cradle I'd be better off. The *world*'d be better off. Hell, I think death is a wonderful thing."

Contrary to his mother's fears that these words will increase her son's worries, David considers his father and his thoughts as distant allies. Mostly, though, still waiting for a sign, David feels alone.

Some time elapses as David's life follows its regular rhythms. His interest in reading subsides. For his fifteenth birthday, he receives a Remington .22, and David begins to spend his time shooting at tin cans out in the woods. At first he is amused by his dog's reactions to the sound of the gun firing, but slowly, David takes to comforting the dog after each shot; in turn, David feels comforted himself by the contact with the dog. But whenever he returns to the house and sees the once-appealing books, his fears also return.

Seeking to divert her son's troubled thoughts, Mrs. Kern tells David that his grandmother needs him to do a special favor for her: shoot the pigeons in the barn so they won't spoil the Olinger furniture stored there. At first, David refuses, but later he agrees.

In the barn's darkness, David's senses are filled with the smell of old straw and the cooing of the pigeons. Finally, he focuses on the noise to locate his prey. After some unsuccessful attempts, David begins to relish his task. "Standing in the center of the floor, fully master now, disdaining to steady the barrel with anything but his arm, he killed two more. . . . He felt like a beautiful avenger. Out of the shadowy ragged infinity of the vast barn roof these impudent things dared to thrust their heads, presumed to dirty its starred silence with their filthy timorous life, and he cut them off, tucked them back neatly into the silence. He had the sensation of a creator . . . out of each of them he was making a full bird." He soon tires of this new skill, though, and he stops after killing six pigeons.

His mother walks out to meet him and begins to gather the dead pigeons. She insists that David bury them: "They're your kill. And be sure to make the hole deep enough. . . ." After he digs the hole, David realizes he has never seen a bird up close. "The feathers were more wonderful than dog's hair, for each filament was shaped within the shape of the feather, and the feathers in turn were trimmed to fit a pattern that flowed without error across the bird's body."

David places the birds in the deep hole. As he does so, the gesture or sign he has sought materializes: "crusty coverings were lifted from him, and with a feminine, slipping sensation along his nerves that seemed to give the air hands, he was robed in this certainty: that the God who had lavished such craft upon these worthless birds would not destroy His whole Creation by refusing to let David live forever." ❀

List of Characters in
"Pigeon Feathers"

David Kern, as he approaches his fifteenth birthday, fills his time with reflections on death and the existence of God.

George Kern, David's father, teaches at a school in the nearby town of Olinger. George, originally from the city, appears somewhat out of place on a farm; he concentrates on the practical, "chemical" side of life.

Elsie Kern, David's mother, prompted their return to the farm where she grew up. Unlike George, Elsie focuses on the soul present in every creature, even in the earth itself.

Granmom, Elsie's mother, suffers from Parkinson's disease. Her infirmity and age are a source of considerable irritation to Elsie. ❀

Critical Views on
"Pigeon Feathers"

LARRY E. TAYLOR ON THE HEBRAIC-CHRISTIAN
TRADITION

[In his chapter entitled "Primary Tensions: Eden and the Fall,
Swain and Sophisticate, Farm and Town in Updike's Early
Work," Larry E. Taylor traces the Hebraic-Christian tradition
present in David's struggle with faith and his fear of death.
Taylor also contrasts the roles of David's mother and father in
this battle.]

In contrast to the mother's persistent pastoral orientation, the boy and
the father sought escape from the farm. The mother, in her love of the
land, is aligned with the traditional dream of "Eden before the Fall,"
when man and nature were in harmony. The father, with his chemistic
reasoning, his urban orientation, and his conventional faith, is somewhat closer to the orthodox tradition.

The question of David's faith and his fear of death is resolved
through a strange union of 1) an act of killing, and 2) a subsequent
transcendental insight into the unity of the universe. He is assigned the
task of killing pigeons in the old barn where unused furniture is stored.
With a rifle, he pumps bullets into the pigeons as they flee through a
small round hole high in the barn wall. The rifle, the hole, the boy's age
all have Freudian connotations. But more important is the sensation of
pleasure derived from the violent act of killing: "He felt like a beautiful
avenger." "He had the sensation of a creator." Like the violent act of the
stoning in *The Poorhouse Fair*, the violent act of shooting the pigeons
unites the boy with death, sin, evil—initiating him into "the Order of
Sinners," the race. Like the pastoral hero's initiation in Hawthorne's
"My Kinsman, Major Molineux," David's destructive act paradoxically
becomes salvational. The paradox is essentially part of the Hebraic-
Christian tradition associated with concepts such as "the fortunate
Fall," death as a prerequisite for life, and loss as a prerequisite for gain.
Having created death through the act of shooting, the boy achieves
transcendental insight through contemplation of his kill. Significantly,
his mother rather than his father arrives to help him bury the birds.
They choose a plot of ground "too steep to plant and mow" where

"wild strawberries grew in the tangled grass." The mother, the pre-lapsarian pastoralist, makes the boy bury the birds alone: "While he went to the tool shed for the shovel, she went into the house. Unlike her, she did not look up, either at the orchard to the right of her or at the meadow on her left, but instead held her head rigidly, tilted a little, as if listening to the ground." In the face of death (the slain pigeons are like the slain deer in Shakespeare's Arden Forest), the pastoralist must face very real anti-pastoral facts of life. The mother's orchards and meadows have been penetrated by sin, evil, and death. In minutely examining the "geometrical tides" of the feathers, the boy feels that the patterns and rhythms seem to have been "executed in a controlled rapture." In death the birds become beautiful; in their beauty, they become life-affirming, and salvational.

—Larry E. Taylor, *Pastoral and Anti-Pastoral Patterns in John Updike's Fiction* (Carbondale, Ill.: Southern Illinois University Press, 1971): pp. 57–58.

RACHAEL C. BURCHARD ON CHRISTIANITY'S FAILURE IN THE STORY

[In the chapter on Updike's short stories in her book *John Updike: Yea Sayings*, Rachael C. Burchard singles out "Pigeon Feathers" as an example of "Updike's theme of man's confusion." This confusion is seen in David's fear and his questioning God's existence. Burchard argues that young David's crises evoke the failure of Christianity to practice what it preaches.]

Updike's theme of man's confusion resounds. David is confused—man is confused—because of society's failure, religion's failure, and each individual's failure.

The confusion is compounded for the boy when, a few days later, he has a distinct vision of death in which he sees his body slowly pressed and elongated and distorted into the earth's strata. The fear of the cosmos in its magnitude and its limitlessness, a theme which appears in some of the Updike poetry, is repeated. One of the consolations offered in the poetry is also renewed. In "Mobile of Birds" man is consoled by the fact that even though he is almost too tiny in relation to the universe to be significant, he is essential just as the single bird is necessary to perfect balance of the mobile. An impression similar to this finally makes its way through the confusion and fear; David feels "his first spark of comfort—too small to be crushed."

This conclusion is the beginning of the boy's climb out of the dungeon of despair toward the bright assurance with which the story finally ends. Up to this point he has not discussed his frantic terror. Now he goes eagerly to the catechetical class at the Lutheran Church. Confident that the good man in the white collar will comfort him, he bravely asks questions about the resurrection of the body, the dwelling place of the soul after death, and the location of Heaven. The minister studiously avoids answering David's questions, gazing at the boy intently "with an awkward, puzzled flicker of forgiveness, as if there existed a secret between them that David was violating." There is created among the children a sense of "naughtiness occurring" as the minister, becoming a coward because he cannot answer the child's questions, transfers his shame to David. There is no better example anywhere in Updike's fiction of the failure of Christianity as man practices it and preaches it. It does not even answer the needs of a sincere, faithful child. As a matter of fact, it makes the child a sinner in the eyes of his peers simply because he yearns for truth. Its answers are inadequate for our time.

—Rachael C. Burchard, *John Updike: Yea Sayings* (Carbondale, Ill.: Southern Illinois University Press, 1971): pp. 148–49.

KATHLEEN VERDUIN ON UPDIKE'S MALE CHARACTERS

[Kathleen Verduin has also published critical studies on Dante and several medieval themes. In this essay, she bases her arguments on the 17th-century Protestant tradition of transferring priestly authority to the father. Focusing on the young David Kern of "Pigeon Feathers," this passage from Verduin's study concentrates on the need for divine manifestation to prove God's existence.]

From the earliest stories, Updike's characters long for a physical and tangible manifestation of the divine. The boy David, in "Pigeon Feathers," goes through motions easy to imagine in a seventeenth-century Puritan writer: "David prayed to be reassured. Though the experiment frightened him, he lifted his hands, high in the darkness above his face, and begged Christ to touch them. Not hard or long: the faintest, quickest grip would be final for a lifetime. His hands waited in the air, itself a substance, which seemed to move through his fingers; or was it the pressure of his pulse? He returned his hands to beneath the covers uncertain if they had been touched or not. For would not Christ's touch *be* infinitely gentle?" Like many things in the story, David's longing for palpable reassurance is paradigmatic, adumbrating the behavior of many of Updike's later and older characters. Even though the patriarchal voice of Karl Barth condemns theological searches for "proof that God exists in the manner of created things," Updike comments [in his essay "Faith in Search of Understanding"], "such, we must weakly confess, is the proof that we hoped for." The doubting temperament that hungers for what the Puritans called "experimental knowledge"—the knowledge verified by the heart's subjective perceptions—will be alert to manifestation of the divine presence. Updike's work is therefore predictably emblematic. His own family, the author says, was "inclined to examine everything for God's fingerprints." In Updike, what is ordinary may quickly turn into an epiphany and no phenomenon is therefore too small to merit attention. For the young minister in "Dentistry and Doubt," even his toothbrush "on good days presented itself as an acolyte of matinal devotion." In "Pigeon Feathers," David's quest for faith is at least momentarily resolved by the intricacy of birds' feathers: "God who had lavished such craft on these worthless birds would not destroy His whole creation by refusing to let David live forever." In this sacramental view, the outward and sensible sign acts as a manifestation of the divine if properly understood: "Just as a piece of turf torn from a meadow becomes a *gloria* when drawn by Dürer" ("The Blessed Man of Boston, My Grandmother's Thimble, and Fanning Island," *Pigeon Feathers*). Updike's characters are accordingly sensitive to the appearances of things and the possible meaning of those appearances; and their eagerness for symbol and emblem is, I think, directly related to problems more central in their lives. As has been charged against Hawthorne's male characters, Updike's protagonists too seem passive and indecisive, as though waiting to be told what to do—as indeed, in a certain sense, they are. For decisions, in Updike's men, are rarely made rationally; instead, their choices often come as a result of some event, some fleeting impression which may be taken as a sign.

—Kathleen Verduin, "Fatherly Presences: John Updike's Place in a Protestant Tradition" in *Critical Essays on John Updike,* William R. Macnaughton, ed. (Boston, Mass.: G. K. Hall and Co., 1982): pp. 261–62.

ARTHUR MIZENER ON THE VERBAL BRILLIANCE OF THE STORY

[Arthur Mizener has published on a wide range of literary figures, including Robert Penn Warren, Vladimir Nabokov, and Ford Madox Ford. In this review, published shortly after *Pigeon Feathers and Other Stories* appeared, Mizener praises the collection of stories and states that it is clear proof of Updike's maturation as a writer. Referring to Updike as "the most talented writer of his age," Mizener attributes to Updike qualities of insight and a "power to dazzle."]

His love of words and ideas for their own sake is almost Joycean, and he has often imitated Joyce in the almost mechanical way of someone doing an exercise in a creative-writing class: How his virtuosity must have charmed his writing teachers! His evident schoolbrightness and the first class education it brought him provided every opportunity for the over-development of his onomastic tendencies. They are most obvious in his verse ("Conceptually a blob, / the knob / is a smallish object which, / hitched / to a larger, / acts as verger"), but they are present also in his fiction, a constant pleasure to anyone who enjoys watching an artist at work.

Verbal brilliance of this kind, however, can be a danger for a writer of fiction. The young man who, under various names, is the hero of the stories in "Pigeon Feathers" says of one of his unknown rivals, "he would wear eyebrow-style glasses, be a griper, have some not quite negotiable talent, like playing the clarinet or drawing political cartoons," thus nicely illustrating his author's highly negotiable talent for adorning his stories with a cosmatesque surface of very great and radically irrelevant decorative charm.

—Arthur Mizener, Review of *Pigeon Feathers and Other Stories* in *The New York Times Book Review* (18 March 1962). Reprinted as "Behind the Dazzle Is a Knowing Eye" in *Critical Essays on John Updike*, William R. Macnaughton, ed. (Boston, Mass.: G. K. Hall and Co., 1982): p. 45.

ROBERT DETWEILER ON INDIVIDUAL FAITH

[Robert Detweiler, a professor at Emory University, is the author of many critical studies, including *Story, Sign, and Self*. Detweiler argues that David's self-imposed status of refugee accentuates his spiritual crisis. In this extract, he discusses the catharsis occasioned by the killing of the pigeons that fosters David's understanding of death and the existence of God. This is not preaching on Updike's part, according to Detweiler, but merely testimony that spiritual growth is possible.]

The element of displacement is crucial to the story. The move from town to country makes David a self-styled geographical refugee; but, above all, it underscores his condition as a spiritual outsider. But that isolation changes when he learns that all men appear to be outsiders—that religion is an elaborate ruse designed not to help one face death honestly but to cushion its reality. In the town, furthermore, one is sufficiently occupied to avoid a contemplation of death; but, in the country, close to what should be the healing power of nature, one is drawn by the proximity of the soil to darker thoughts of death and decay. The arguments between David's parents about natural and organic farming amplify, for his distressed ears, his anxiety; for the strife about what kills the soil leads him to additional visions of the grave. In his hypertense condition, even the outhouse, resting above the pit of decomposing feces, triggers a horrid nightmare glimpse of a dying universe.

Personal participation in death restores—or first creates—David's faith. The killing of the pigeons is a catharsis, a cleansing involvement in violence and destruction that is a microform of the Classical tragic mode. But David, who feels like an avenger in the excitement of the shooting, also attains a measure of understanding about the meaning of death and of divinity in the scheme of being: "He had the sensation of a creator; . . . out of each of them he was making a full bird." The analogy, of course, is that man likewise is somehow fulfilled through death and that God in allowing death is not permitting a catastrophic absurdity but a good and necessary consummation. The horror of infinity changes to a trust in its intelligent perfection, unarticulated as its form may be. In the final words of the story, David is "robed in certainty: that the God who had lavished such craft upon these worthless birds would not destroy His whole creation by refusing to let David live forever."

The culminating action and the conclusion of the story sound suspiciously like a fictional updating of the Scholastic argument from design for God's existence, and one should not be inattentive to the possible irony in the whole performance. After all, the line of logic from a half-dozen dead pigeons to a boy's new assurance of personal immortality is broken by numerous forensic short circuits. But that philosophical argument is not the point of the story, nor should it be the center of criticism regarding the story. The point is that Updike, through symbolic action and analogy, has written a moving narrative that does not presume to convince one of the truth of religious faith but that does testify to an individual's achievement of it.

—Robert Detweiler, *John Updike* (Boston, Mass.: Twayne Publishers, 1984): pp. 49–50.

STEVEN M. CHANLEY ON PERSONAL MYTHOLOGY

[Steven M. Chanley develops an extensive list of the steps that young David Kern takes to order his own universe, or, as Chanley sees it, to adopt his own mythology. In this excerpt, he examines the final and crucial step in this process in which David synthesizes the many thoughts and doubts found in his spiritual darkness. By burying the pigeons, Chanley says, David lifts himself out of existential uncertainty to see a new order.]

There is some obvious validity, it behooves us to discuss, to the contention that David's final task is archetypal, in that his entering the dark barn, conquering the fear of death, and emerging into the sunlight represents the archetypal hero's requisite journey to the underworld (death) and subsequent return (rebirth). However, such a treatment of his task fails to acknowledge the precedent set by the other darkroom/beam-of-light metaphors in the story, in which the darkness doesn't represent death, in the traditional literary sense, but rather earthly life, which is shrouded in the shadows of nontruth. Furthermore, the cyclical progression of the monomythic hero's journey, of which the death/rebirth phase is a part, is not apparent in "Pigeon Feathers."

In any event, although his final step toward maturation is successfully completed by killing the pigeons in the barn, David has yet to completely synthesize his revelations into a mythology that helps him to conceptualize the universal order and "build his fortress against death" until he buries the pigeons. He begins that synthesis, however, immediately upon emerging from the barn, when he incorporates some of his father's stoical acceptance of death into his own beliefs. That is suggested not only by the facts that David uses the term "poor devils" and carries his gun in a careless manner, which are made explicit characteristics of his father in the story, but also by his mother's comment when he emerges from the barn: "Don't smirk. You look like your father." (His father, incidentally, is so thoroughly comfortable with the idea of death, that his favorite expression is "That reminds me of death.") Nonetheless, it is the burial of the pigeons that marks the epiphany in David, which results in his adoption of a mythology or system for ordering the universe.

While preparing to lay the birds in a freshly dug hole, David marvels at the infinite detail, irridescent luster, and exquisite beauty inherent to the pigeons' lifeless bodies.

> . . . across the surface of the infinitely adjusted yet somehow effortless mechanics of the feathers played idle designs of color, no two alike, designs executed, it seemed, in a controlled rapture, with a joy that hung level in the air above and behind him.

"Yet," David realizes, despite the sublime intricacy with which these pigeons are wrought, "these birds [breed] in the millions and [are] exterminated as pests." This revelation, above everything else, causes him to realize that no matter how special he had previously assumed himself to be, he must, like even the most beautiful creatures, of which there are many, succumb to death, which is as much a part of nature as life. With this epiphany, "crusty coverings" are lifted from David, and a passage follows that is perhaps the key to the story, insofar as understanding the mythology that David adopts following his revelation.

> . . . he was robed in this certainty: that the God who had lavished such craft upon these worthless birds would not destroy His whole Creation by refusing to let David live forever.

His "crusty coverings," in other words, give way to a robe of certainty, which represents his personal mythology. The passage is purposely ambiguous to lend itself to two related interpretations, both of which apparently illustrate David's conception of the universal order: one interpretation is that God will refuse to let David live forever, because not refusing to do so would destroy His whole creation, of which death is an integral part; the other interpretation is that the refusal to let David live forever is of no consequence—it will not destroy the works of a God whose creation is so glorious that even its worthless creatures are beautiful. The importance of David's loss of individuality, which gradually came about along his various steps, is apparent in this universal scheme, which is something of a conglomerate of his mother's reverence of nature and his father's wholehearted acceptance of death.

—Steven M. Chanley, "Quest for Order in 'Pigeon Feathers': Updike's Use of Christian Mythology," *Arizona Quarterly* 43, no. 3 (Autumn 1987): pp. 261–62.

John Updike on the Story's Background

[As if rewriting a scene from "Pigeon Feathers," in this extract from his memoirs John Updike explains his views on religion and the existence of God by relating the syllogism he formed for the purpose.]

Early in my adolescence, trapped within the airtight case for atheism, I made this logical formulation:

1. If God does not exist, the world is a horror-show.
2. The world is not a horror-show.
3. Therefore, God exists.

The second premise, of course, is the weaker; newspapers and biology lessons daily suggest that it *is* a horror show, of landslides and plagues and massacres and falling airplanes and incessant carnivorousness. And of—we cannot but be especially conscious these days—venereal disease: what more fiendish proof of cosmic irresponsibility than a Nature which, having invented sex as a way to mix genes, then permits to arise, amid all its perfumed and hypnotic inducements to mate, a tireless tribe of spirochetes and viruses that torture and kill us for following orders? Yet this and all bad news merits reporting because our general expectation is for good: an instinctive vision of health and peace underlies our horror stories. Existence itself does not feel horrible; it feels like an ecstasy, rather, which we only have to be still to experience. Habit and accustomedness have painted over pure gold with a dull paint that can, however, be scratched away, to reveal the shining under-base. The world is good, our intuition is, confirming its Creator's appraisal as reported in the first chapter of Genesis.

During that same adolescence, I reluctantly perceived of the Christian religion I had been born into that almost no one believed it, believed it really—not its ministers, nor its pillars like my father and his father before him. Though signs of belief (churches, public prayers, mottos on coins) existed everywhere, when you moved toward Christianity it disappeared, as fog solidly opaque in the distance thins to transparency when you walk into it. I decided I nevertheless *would* believe. I found a few authors, a very few—Chesterton, Eliot, Una-muno, Kierkegaard, Karl Barth—who helped me believe. Under the shelter (like the wicker chairs on the side porch) that I improvised from their pages I have lived my life. I rarely read them now; my life is mostly lived. God is the God of the living, though His priests and executors, to keep order and to force the world into a convenient mould, will always want to make Him the God of the dead, the God who chastises life and forbids and says No. What I felt, in that basement Sunday school of Grace Lutheran Church in Shillington, was a clumsy attempt to extend a Yes, a blessing, and I accepted that blessing, offering in return only a nickel a week and my art, my poor little art.

—John Updike, *Self-Consciousness* (New York: Alfred A. Knopf, 1989): pp. 229–31.

Plot Summary of
"Packed Dirt, Churchgoing,
A Dying Cat, A Traded Car"

This is the last entry in *Pigeon Feathers and Other Stories*. It first appeared in the *New Yorker* on December 16, 1961, and is also part of the collection *Olinger Stories*. The story has four separate but conceptually joined parts that are united in the mind and memories of the narrator, the same David Kern from "Pigeon Feathers," now an adult.

The first section begins with David's comments on humans' fascination with the "sight of bare earth that has been smoothed and packed firm by the passage of human feet." David frames his series of narratives with the image of packed dirt, since it reminds him of the well-worn paths and playgrounds, the times and spaces in childhood "when one communes with dirt down among the legs, as it were, of presiding fatherly presences."

In contrast, as an adult, David's present image of packed dirt is the lot next door where his neighbor's house recently stood. The house was sacrificed, he explains, so that bulldozers could flatten the parcel and open it as a road to summer traffic. His son cries from the bulldozers' noise, and David and his neighbors complain about the unsightliness of the vacant lot. When David notices a new foot-worn path already developing through the lot's weeds, he is at once reassured. "This small modification, this modest work of human erosion, seemed precious to me not only because it recalled, in the slope and set of the dirt, a part of the path that long ago had led down from my parents' back yard to the high-school softball field. It seemed precious because it had been achieved accidentally, and had about it that repose of grace that is beyond willing." This represents for David "a sense of human legacy" in the face of planned destruction.

Next, in the section "Churchgoing," David remembers the time when regular attendance at church was important to him. For David, going to church services ranks higher than anything else democracy might have to offer: "Indeed, it is the most available democratic experience. We vote less than once a year. Only in church and at the polls are we actually given our supposed value, the soul-unit of one, with its noumenal arithmetic of equality: one equals one equals one."

David's interest in regular church attendance flowered with adolescence. Prior to that he was content to follow his mother's example of believing in phenomena and staying home on Sunday mornings. In Lent, though, David ushered at church with his father. At that time he found the inner space of the church especially appealing: "There was a strong sepia flavor of early Christianity: a minority flock furtively gathered within the hostile enormity of a dying, sobbing empire." This ushering offered David the pleasure of sitting next to his father, but in his opinion, the same delight could be dangerous as well, since "to usher at a church mixes us with the angels."

Unlike the countryside of David's youth, Manhattan created a perpetual atmosphere of Lent for him. Despite this, David explains, he "never attended the same church two Sundays in succession, for fear I would become known, and be expected." In contrast, his church-going on an island in the Caribbean was recognized, and his identity was marked by the very color of his skin. The services, David thought, were exceedingly long and the hymns resonated with both "British accent and Negro elision." But there he discovered he could escape in and out of the windows. After all, Kern reminded himself, "God made the word, Aquinas says, in play."

The section "A Dying Cat" shifts in time and place to Oxford, England, where David and his wife are expecting the birth of their daughter. David dutifully attends to his wife but was sent home by the hospital staff. On that last day in March, David looks forward to welcoming his daughter in the same month as his own birth. Sometime that night around midnight, he goes for a walk near their apartment and notices a shadow move in the middle of the street.

At first, he is horrified by the shape, because it seems the size of a baby. On closer inspection, David realizes it is a tabby cat that was hit by a car. The cat is near death as David moves it carefully. "The only sound between us was my crooning as I carried it to the side of the street and laid it behind the nearest hedge." The cat has a collar; it must be a loved pet, David assumes. But he also worries that someone viewing his movements might interpret them as those of a poacher or a trespasser.

David returns home in search of a pen and paper. Removing his blood-stained glove, he begins to write, "explaining that I had found this cat in the middle of the street, still alive, and that I had put it behind this hedge to be safe. . . . After some deliberation, I signed my name and address." David leaves the note with the cat, returns home, and sleeps fitfully. Waking from a dream, he dresses, goes out, and calls the hospital from a public phone. "A chirping voice, after some rummaging in the records, told me that several hours ago, in the first hour of April (in the United States it was still March), a perfect female infant had been born. To me." The next day he returns to the hedge, and finds neither the cat nor his note.

The principal tale in the four-part story unfolds in "A Traded Car." On their return from England, David and his wife purchased a 1955 Ford. The sturdy and loyal car never complained, according to David, in the six years that they used it. However, David focuses on the events that took place in the month before he traded in this faithful mechanical friend for a newer model.

The story begins at a party where David finds himself dancing with a woman who is not his wife. He turns his partner's clumsy lurching into an opportunity to kiss her palm. This contact sends him into a higher realm: "Her back seemed mysteriously taut and hard; the body of a strange woman retains more of its mineral content, not being transmuted, through familiarity, into pure emotion." They dance, then leave to sit and talk, and all the while his partner's soft grip on his thumbs makes David tremble and pant.

Returning home, David and his wife, after checking in on their four children, exchange the party's tensions for physical contact. David is not sure why his wife does not ignore his presence, as has become her habit; "Alcohol, with its loosening effect, touches women more deeply than men in this respect; or perhaps, like a matched pair of tuning forks, I had set her vibrating. Irritated by whatever illicit stimulations, we took it out on each other."

Their lovemaking leaves David in the throes of insomnia, his thoughts filled with his dance partner of the evening. He remembers from his many Sunday school sessions the lesson "in which Jesus says that to lust after a woman in thought is the same as committing adultery." This and scores of other thoughts pile into his mind. In a passage that reminds the reader of the younger David Kern of

"Pigeon Feathers," David the adult reverts to prayer: "The dark vibrating air of my bedroom seemed the dust of my grave; the dust went up and up and I prayed upward into it, prayed, prayed for a sign, any glimmer at all, any microscopic loophole of chink in the chain of evidence, and saw none."

But David's insomnia and guilty thoughts lead him in a different direction than the one the adolescent David took. Now his troubled mind negates God: "Each second my agony went unanswered justifies it more certainly: the God who permitted me this fear was unworthy of existence. Each instant my horror was extended amplified God's non-existence...." His self-imposed agony is so acute that David wakes up his wife Elaine to transfer his fears to her.

The following day is Saturday and David's birthday. But his malaise from the evening before continues: "Friends visited, and for the first time truly in my life I realized that each face is suppressing knowledge of an immense catastrophe; our faces are dams that wrinkle under the strain." In the early evening, David receives a call from his mother. Expecting her to wish him a happy birthday, David instead hears her say that his father is very ill. "Instantly I was relieved. The weight on me rolled away. All day death had been advancing under cover and now it had struck. . . . My father had engaged the enemy and it would be defeated."

The bad news rejuvenates David. He enjoys his birthday party, takes his children to church the next day, and decides at the last minute to drive to his parents' home in the old Ford. Outside of Boston, David picks up a young sailor to join him for the long ride.

The sailor, tanned from his stay in Key West, has returned to his home in Salem to visit his parents and his girlfriend. As David and the sailor talk, David learns that the young man is waiting anxiously for the end of his Navy tour so he can marry his girl and start a life together.

The sailor asks about David's work, initiating a telling exchange:
"'What do you write?'
"'Oh, whatever comes into my head.'
"'What's the point?'
"'I don't know,' I told him. 'I wish I did.'"

David drops the young sailor off near the New Jersey turnpike and continues his trip to Pennsylvania on his own. Once in his home state, the familiar sights reassure David. Parking the Ford in his parents' yard, David sees his mother approach. She greets him by saying: "Daddy says he's lost all his faith."

That night, David sleeps badly. He is cold, and he misses his wife and children. The next day, however, begins as a bright and shiny spring day. David insists on driving his mother into town in the Ford. They meet with the doctor in charge of his father's case, and then, while his mother runs an errand, David goes in the town library and seeks out the many books that colored his childhood. "I never thought to look for the section of the shelves where my own few books would be placed. They were not me. They were my children, mysterious and self-willed."

Then, entering the hospital with his mother, David remembers another April day when she accompanied him to the hospital to have his tonsils removed. This time his mother knows her way around without depending on direction from either her husband or her son. Her demeanor has changed as well: "As I followed her through the linoleum maze, my mother's shoulders seemed already to have received the responsible shawl of widowhood."

His old image of his father is also transformed when he sees the pajamas his father is wearing. When the older man laments never giving his son an original thought, David disagrees, saying: "You taught me two things. Always butter bread toward the edges because enough gets in the middle anyway, and No matter what happens to you, it'll be a new experience." Instead of consoling his father, David's reminiscence provokes another worry. His father fears that, in his absence, his wife will "crack up the car." David notices his mother's quiet tears, and feels even more helpless toward his father. "I wanted to speak, to say how I needed him and to beg him not to leave me, but there were no words, no form of words available in our tradition."

A young girl from the Lutheran Home Missions enters the room to give David's father a pamphlet that contains comforting religious passages. The nervous banter delivered by the elder Mr. Kern confuses the girl; each time Mr. Kern says, "That's awfully nice of you," she resorts to her well-rehearsed routine. David's father, however, perks up his son and his wife with this chatter. Mr. Kern also has kind words for his son: "He told me I was a good son and a good father; he clasped my hand. I felt I would ascend straight north from his touch."

David drives his mother back home and says goodbye, once again put at ease by the familiarity of the surroundings. On the trip back, though, he has no companion to break the monotony. "Distance grew thicker and thicker; the intricate and effortful mechanics of the engine, the stellar infinity of explosive sparks needed to drive it, passed into my body, and wearied me." Dreamlike thoughts fill his senses until he realizes that the Ford had "evolved into something soft and organic and consciously brave." The car, steady and safe, returns David to his yard and his house.

Just like his father did many times, he is about to trade in a car. As he reflects on this, David realizes that this same car would soon be gone, "dismissed without a blessing, a kiss, a testament, or any ceremony of farewell. We in America need ceremonies, is I suppose, sailor, the point of what I have written." ❀

List of Characters in
"Packed Dirt, Churchgoing,
A Dying Cat, A Traded Car"

David Kern is the narrator of this multi-part tale, the adult extension of the adolescent seen in "Pigeon Feathers." He describes a series of episodes from childhood into adulthood. The issues of God and death once again surface in David's life.

Elaine Kern is David's wife and the mother of his four children; she figures only as a subject, a backdrop to some of the related events.

Mrs. Kern, David's mother, asks her son to come home because of his father's grave illness. She reminds David of the past, as well as of the immanence of future changes.

Mr. Kern, David's father, is dying from a serious heart condition; he and David share a tender and important moment when Mr. Kern essentially bids his son goodbye for the last time.

The *young sailor* hitches a ride with David Kern. They talk about the sailor's plans to marry his girlfriend and about David's work as a writer. This exchange causes David to reflect on the reasons he writes. ❀

Critical Views on
"Packed Dirt, Churchgoing,
A Dying Cat, A Traded Car"

ALICE AND KENNETH HAMILTON ON "SUPERNATURAL
MAIL"

[Alice and Kenneth Hamilton have published several articles jointly on John Updike and Samuel Beckett. In this
chapter of their joint project, they analyze the expression
"supernatural mail" that Updike uses in "Packed Dirt,
Churchgoing, A Dying Cat, A Traded Car." This section of
their chapter compares the revelation experienced by
David Kern at the end of "Pigeon Feathers" with the adult
Kern's dealings with birth and death.]

On the "endless" return drive, David's old car seems to take over
with a will of its own, "though its soul the driver had died." His
safe homecoming is described in these words: "Above my back yard
the stars were frozen in place, and the shapes of my neighbors'
houses wore the wonder that children induce by whirling." The
story ends with David's regretful reflection about how the car that
carried him home so faithfully will soon be turned in, like so many
others before, "dismissed without a blessing, a kiss, a testament, or
any ceremony of farewell." Then follows the final apostrophe to the
sailor concerning the need for ceremony in America.

David Kern's four-section story does not culminate, as "Pigeon
Feathers" does, in an ecstasy of revelation. Maturity is not childhood, and it has different needs. Comprehensiveness of vision is
demanded by adult responsibilities, while intense feeling marks
childhood experience.

David Kern the man gains the sustaining vision allowing him to
accept the fact that matter has both radiance and darkness. His
birthday comes at the "dull season" of the year "during which
Spring is gathering the mineral energy to make the resurrection
that the church calendar seizes upon as conveniently emblematic."
He has known this season as the bringer of birth and death: once
when his daughter was born and a cat died on an English street,

and now again when his birthday brings word of his father's possibly fatal illness. On both occasions supernatural mail has arrived making possible "that repose of grace that is beyond willing," bringing peaceful sleep, release from the fear of death, and a safe return to his own back yard, illumined by wonder. Supernatural mail always says, *Run on home.* But where is home? Things compete, and earthly affection is divided. Those we love die. Life moves on, and time will not wait for us. Ultimately, we are sustained only by that radiance which can take us through death to resurrection.

David trusts his father's faith to defeat the enemy death. It is true that his father, apparently, has lost his faith. Yet Hooker's words quoted in "Dentistry and Doubt" hold good. "I grant we are apt, prone, and ready, to forsake God; but is God as ready to forsake us?" In Alton, the doctor, explaining George Kern's illness to David, points out that the obstruction affecting the heart is "in one of these little vessels on the outside, luckily for your dad." The "heart," then, is not fatally "obstructed" in its relation to God, and loss of faith is external only. David knows that his father still communicates the radiance of faith that has power to defeat death. So when he receives his farewell blessing and handclasp, David comments, "I felt I would ascend straight north from his touch." The background to this reference is the biblical association of God's dwelling-place with the north, as described in the Psalms:

> *Mount Zion, in the far north,*
> *the city of the great King.*
> *Within her citadel God*
> *has shown himself a sure defense.* (Ps. 48:2–3)

Receiving his father's blessing, David realizes that his father is one of those who can "ascend the hill of the Lord" and there "receive blessing" (Ps. 24:3, 5).

—Alice and Kenneth Hamilton, *The Elements of John Updike* (Grand Rapids, Mich.: William B. Eerdmans, 1970): pp. 98–99.

[In the fourth chapter of her thematic study, the published
version of her doctoral thesis, Joyce B. Markle examines the
many representations of the mother in Updike's fiction. In this
excerpt, she begins with two mothers from *Pigeon Feathers
and Other Stories*—Mrs. Dow and Mrs. Kern—and another
mother from *The Centaur*, Mrs. Robinson. Markle then contrasts these with the elder Mrs. Kern in the fourth section of
"Packed Dirt, Churchgoing, A Dying Cat, A Traded Car." Here
she argues that the mother figure has evolved from weaker
roles into this more assertive one where the elderly mother
shows strengthened character.]

The mother in "Pigeon Feathers," *The Centaur*, and "Flight" has a
pleading manner, a besieged look; she seems harassed and defeated; her
prose style has a slight whining quality.

> "George, don't you read the papers? Don't you know that between the
> chemical fertilizers and the bug sprays we'll all be dead in ten years?"
> ⟨"Pigeon Feathers"⟩
>> "You're killing *earth*worms, George!" ⟨"Pigeon Feathers"⟩
>> "Your father was a disappointed *man*. Why should *you* be disap-
> pointed?" ⟨*The Centaur*⟩
>> "Mother, stop hanging on my *back*! Why don't you go to *bed*?"
> ⟨"Pigeon Feathers"⟩
>> "Pop, can't you wait until they're out of the house before you
> start tormenting the bread?"⟨*The Centaur*⟩

Yet she has already developed the skill in family drama that marks
Joey's mother ⟨in *Of the Farm*⟩. Angry at her husband's attitudes
toward farming ⟨in "Pigeon Feathers"⟩, David's mother bangs a cup in
the kitchen and cries, "You talked Pop into his grave and now you'll kill
me. Go ahead, George, more power to you."

We see her a few years later as Allen's mother in "Flight." The pitch of
her whine is changing, becoming sharper. "You'll never learn, you'll
stick and die in the dirt just like I'm doing. Why should you be better
than your mother?" And the hostility towards her son's female friends
has emerged with bitter force. "Don't go with little women, Allen. It
puts you too close to the ground."

The short story, "A Traded Car," views the household at a time a few years prior to the setting of the fourth novel. The son is married but the father is still living, though hospitalized with chronic heart disease. In this story we seem to see the mother in transition between the younger, weaker woman and the assertive elderly widow. Blushing and embarrassed, she tells her son, visiting because of his father's illness, "Daddy says he's lost all his faith." But the son notices the authoritative way she leads him through the hospital corridors. Her coming widowhood is altering and strengthening her character. "My mother's shoulders seemed already to have received the responsible shawl of widowhood." Her sarcastic humor is also beginning to develop. When her son asks about an old girl friend, she replies in mock disappointment, "Oh, dear, I thought you came all this way to see your poor old father and all you care about is seeing—." Her husband fears she will crack up the car and worries, "I don't want anything to happen to your mother." "The car, you mean," she jibes; "It's a sin, the way he worships that car." By the time she appears in *Of the Farm*, her personality has matured into the tough-spoken but thin-skinned Mrs. Robinson. Forced into the man's role of head of her house and property, she has even borrowed some of her husband's personality, such as his strange self-deprecatory but bullying manner.

—Joyce B. Markle, *Fighters and Lovers: Theme in the Novels of John Updike* (New York: New York University Press, 1973): pp. 84–86.

DONALD J. GREINER ON DAVID KERN'S RELIGIOUS CRISIS

[Donald J. Greiner has also published critical essays on James Dickey and Frederick Busch. In this excerpt, he discussed the way the mature David Kern has survived his adolescent religious crisis to meet another one, as the contemplation of adultery brings Kern close to despair as he questions the very existence of God. As Greiner further explains, Kern learns lessons along the way.]

Later in the collection, in "Packed Dirt, Churchgoing, A Dying Cat, A Traded Car," we learn that David Kern survives the adolescent religious crisis to become the regular adult churchgoer. But in the last section of this four-part story, he confronts another religious dilemma: Are men judged by the soul's convictions or the body's deeds? Is the sensation of lust the same as the sin of adultery? David now suspects that a universe which would permit adultery would also sanction death—his death. Updike shows that contemplation of annihilation is not limited to the naive questioning of adolescents. David Kern has grown up, but he is still afraid: "I seemed already eternally forgotten. The dark vibrating air of my bedroom seemed the dust of my grave; the dust went up and up and I prayed upward into it, prayed, prayed for a sign, any glimmer at all, any microscopic loophole or chink in the chain of evidence, and saw none." The minute intricacies of pigeon feathers will not help him this time. Reasoning that the God who permits his fear is unworthy of existence, he totters on the brink of despair. David has lost touch with the packed-dirt paths made by children and suggestive of grace.

Thus he has little to answer his mother with when, visiting her and his hospitalized father, she tells him that Mr. Kern no longer believes. Her telephone call on his birthday turns out to be a summons to death. Unexpectedly, he feels relief at the message, for he still has a childlike confidence in his father as a man who can defeat all adversaries. How, then, can he accept his dad's loss of faith? He learns that the beauty of his father's life is that he gives others faith, not so much in the specifics of religious mystery but in the grace of a job well done. David hurries to help his sick father but leaves buoyed by the old man's humor. His journey back home in an old car about to be traded is a renewal of the soul's voyage. Death and life are one, a truth he learns in England when he helps a dying cat on the night of his child's birth and which is reinforced here when the father falls ill on David's birthday. Mr. Kern may have lost religious faith, but as the doctor points out, the old man's heart is not yet blocked. Thus the strong gain from the weak: "I felt I would ascend straight north from his touch."

More important, he learns a lesson which sustains him as a writer and which in turn supports us. Earlier, he is asked by a hitchhiking sailor to explain the reason for writing. He cannot answer then, but now, following the visit to the ailing father, he can: "We in America need ceremonies, is I suppose, sailor, the point of what I have written." His first crucial ceremony takes place when, as a boy, he handles the dead pigeons. But as an adult, he needs more than one revelation. Grown now from adolescent to author, he uses his art to keep us in touch with our rituals, our memories, ourselves. Writers preserve the ceremonies which sustain humanity. They show how things which have served well in the past are not to be sloughed off in the present as easily as a traded car, "dismissed without a blessing, a kiss, a testament, or any ceremony of farewell." Driving back through the dark, he is consoled as his old car brings him safely home to a vision of permanent stars in the black night of the soul.

—Donald J. Greiner, *The Other John Updike* (Athens: Ohio University Press, 1981): pp. 114–16.

JANE BARNES ON THE WEAKNESS OF THE STORY

[Here, along with analyses of other Updike stories such as those collected in *Too Far to Go* and *Problems*, Jane Barnes considers "Packed Dirt, Churchgoing, A Dying Cat, A Traded Car" as an example of Updike's control of structure at its weakest. In this excerpt Barnes points to the connection between the author's life and art.]

These distractions get the upper hand when the author's moral grasp of his material is weakest. In "Packed Dirt, Churchgoing, A Dying Cat, A Traded Car," for instance, the overwriting goes hand in hand with the falsely ancient tone of the young man. He comes home to see his sick father in the hospital, his thoughts coated by a world weariness worthy of a very old person who'd seen nothing but war, torture, and death. In fact, the narrator is a young, sub-urban husband who's seen nothing but peace and domesticity, whose real problem (as he confesses to a hitchhiker) is that he doesn't see the point of his virtuous life. This is not quite the same thing as confronting the void, though there is a tendency in Updike's stories to inflate American boredom into French existen-tialist despair. At his worst, there is more sneakiness than evil in Updike, more opportunism than moral questing in his restless, curious narrator.

Then, too, though the narrator is clearly a self-centered person, it is not clear that his suffering is more than the pinch we all feel trying to live decently with others. His suffering sometimes seems like pure whining—his philosophizing nothing more than a complaint that spouses can cramp a person's sexual style. It is generally assumed that Updike's stories about domestic life are autobiographical. This assumption seems to be made out of a worldly wisdom which allows all sophisticated people to connect what is known about the author through articles (*i.e.*, that Updike has been married, divorced, and recently remarried) and what happens in the fictional life of his central hero (who has been married, divorced, and recently remarried). It *is* hard not to wonder if the narrator hasn't benefited from Updike's possible experience. At the start, the narrator is a timid, even a cowardly man. That he slowly, but surely has his way with women probably has less to do with a change in his personal charm and more with the unadmitted fact that the author's fame made him desirable and gave him unexpected opportunities, ones which Updike passed on to his narrator. There are times when the narrator's cheerlessness about his adulteries seems just insupportable, only explicable by something having been left out—such as the fact that this is not the typical experience of a lusty suburban male, but rather the typical experience of a celebrity who suddenly finds himself in sexual demand. The narrator's depression would be more believable if it *were* openly identified as the cynicism a famous author might feel towards a rise in his desirability that had nothing to do with his true human self.

Yet having made these criticisms, I want to disassociate myself from the knowing, worldly assumption that Updike's work must be autobiographical. I want to consider the role of autobiography in these stories, but I want to do it from the inside out. Instead of talking about them as reflections of the author's life, I want to discuss their importance in his development as a writer.

Updike himself makes the connection between the human content and the author's art. He speaks of his hero's sense of being the "creator" of both his parents and his mistress. From the start, we know the narrator regards women and art as equally mysterious, if not equivalents. We know that women have dominated his experience, that they are the media through which he comes to terms with the past, learns to love and begins to act for himself. When the author refers to the narrator's sense of himself as the artist of his private life, the association of women with art naturally teams up with Updike's identification with his hero. We can take this as the primary, the *essential* starting point of any discussion of the role of autobiography.

—Jane Barnes, "John Updike: A Literary Spider" *Virginia Quarterly Review* 57, no. 1 (Winter 1981). Reprinted in *John Updike*, Harold Bloom, ed. (New York: Chelsea House Publishers, 1987): pp. 121–22.

JOHN UPDIKE ON FAMILY SAYINGS

[In this section of his memoirs, Updike directs a letter to his two grandsons in which he quotes many of the sayings he often heard his own father use. Quite like the scene in the final section of "Packed Dirt, Churchgoing, A Dying Cat, A Traded Car" when the adult David Kern tells his father the ideas he has inherited from him, here Updike mentions two of the same catchphrases along with others of similar ilk.]

Dear boys, the world I grew up in was raw and rough enough to threaten the survival of decent people, who paid their dues, revered their flag, honored God and their parents, tried to do the right thing. How often, in the household of my childhood, did I hear of people trying to do the right thing! That there *was* a right thing seems an old-fashioned notion now; the family I grew up in was so old-fashioned we quoted proverbs aloud, to give each other courage and direction. *Willful waste makes woeful want. A fool and his money are soon parted.* My maternal grandfather would pronounce these in a clear and elocutionary voice made melancholy by the suspicion that no one was listening. My father had evolved minimal consolations, which he often offered aloud: *No matter what happens to you, it will be a new experience. You don't get something for nothing. Dog eat dog.* Sitting in a chair, he would suddenly announce, *I hate everybody,* and a remarkably diverse number of things reminded him, he informed his immediate family, of death. I took these words to be pedagogically offered as a realistic counterbalance to my own innate optimism and capacity for self-serving fantasy. He was a teacher, by instinct as well as fate, and hardly a day goes by that I do not remember his telling me, with a satisfaction so keen as to have cosmic implications, *Water is the great solvent.* Artistically I have lived by his advice in regard to buttering bread: *Butter toward the edges; enough gets in the middle anyway.* My mother had fewer slogans, but in doing research for her often-revised but never-published novel about Ponce de León, she discovered a proverb she said was Spanish but perhaps exists in many languages: *Take what you want and pay the price for it.*

—John Updike, *Self-Consciousness* (New York: Alfred A. Knopf, 1989): pp. 208–9.

Robert M. Luscher on David Kern

[Robert M. Luscher is the author of essays on Updike, J. D. Salinger, and Emily Dickinson. Here, Luscher states that the montage made of the four sections in "Packed Dirt, Church-going, A Dying Cat, A Traded Car" relates either to David Kern's father or his own fatherhood. According to Luscher, the mature Kern seeks some continuity with his past. In this final section of his chapter on ceremonies of farewell, Luscher compares the adult Kern in "A Traded Car" to characters in several other Updike works.]

Ten years older than in "Pigeon Feathers," and now father of four, Kern has become a writer and moved to New England, but still looks back to Olinger as his spiritual center. His montage of recollections is a cyclical journey, wearing a new path through the obstructive rubble of adult life with forays into his past. In his comments on the story's composition, Updike notes how the accumulation of images enhanced his understanding of "Proust's remark about the essence of the writer's task being the perception of connections between unlike things." This "farraginous narrative," he continues, contains "a good deal of conscious art" in the interweaving of themes that "had long been present to me: paternity and death, earth and faith and cars." As distance in time from Olinger increases, so does the "pressure of memory and worry" which spurs the local boy's similar attempt to draw connections and counter loss. Associative memory allows Kern to retravel past incidents and create a new coherence, one that also weaves together many of the collection's persistent themes. "Packed Dirt" not only harmonizes four diverse elements but also produces an even "bigger, better kind of music" in its echoes of the preceding stories. ⟨. . .⟩

The final section, "A Traded Car," chronicles a more significant "ceremony of farewell": the narrator's final trip in his soon-to-be-traded first car, which is linked symbolically with an epoch of his life. Its trading marks a passage, one that Kern memorializes through a journey back to his old Pennsylvania home. Confronted with the conjunction of a flare-up of adulterous longings, his recurrent fear of death, and his father's illness, he realizes that there is only one answer: "run on home" in a quest to banish his fear of death, just as Clyde Behn returns to Olinger to face his "disconsolate youth" and persistent desire. Before he visits the hospital, Kern passes the Alton museum (the same one Peter Caldwell visits in *The Centaur*), recalling how in his youth "the world then seemed an intricate wonder displayed for my delight with no price asked." Such unguarded accessibility, characteristic of Olinger's "incoherent generosity," has since vanished with maturity and responsibility. In the Alton library, Kern seeks continuity with his past, searching in books for date imprints that might indicate when he read them rather than looking for the books he has written that might eventually guarantee immortality. Ultimately, he draws strength from both the locale and from his father's apparent truce with death. Mr. Kern's faith may have slipped somewhat, but his buoyant spirits still convey reassurance to his son, for whom he remains a "presiding fatherly presence," standing between him and death.

Kern's departure recalls a similar one by John Nordholm in "The Happiest I've Been," but his age and the impending car trade clearly signal a departure in a new key. In contrast to Nordholm's sunrise departure for Chicago at the end of *The Same Door*, twilight descends for Kern at the New Jersey border; although he must return north in darkness, he does so with a new ability to face his own dark forebodings. There is both terror and joy, he reflects, in man's marriage to the world; "we bring to it a nature not our bride's," he notes, reconciled to the source of the transforming impulse that wreaks changes on the landscape in the "Packed Dirt" segment. While Nordholm feels a new sense of control at the wheel, since others are trusting him, Kern trusts the car, soon to be part of his past, to guide him back to his present. At the wheel during the final leg of his trip, Kern, in an intensification of his father's attachment to his cars, undergoes a metaphoric death, losing "first, heart, then head, and finally any sense of my body" as he becomes one with the vehicle. Thus, after its final service is performed, he returns reconciled to change but conscious of the need for some further "ceremony of farewell" to mark the passage. Through his art, he performs this ceremony, recapturing the elusive past and successfully preserving a pathway to it that may be travelled perpetually.

"Packed Dirt, Churchgoing, A Dying Cat, A Traded Car," which Updike intended to be the last of his Pennsylvania stories, says his first in a series of farewells to Olinger; subsequent collections concentrate on older characters, take place in other locales, and portray a widening gulf from the past and within marriage. Yet Updike pays homage to Olinger once again when he gathers seven stories from *Pigeon Feathers*, three from *The Same Door*, and one that later appears in *The Music School* into his short story sequence *Olinger Stories: A Selection*. Though initially reluctant to reharvest previously published material, Updike found aesthetic and personal justification to overcome his doubts: "They succumbed to the hope that a concentration of certain images might generate new light, or at least focus more sharply the light already there. . . . I bind these stories together as one ties up a package of love letters that have been returned." In assembling the scattered stories of his local boy into a Bildungsroman, Updike gave formal unity to his Olinger fiction and closed the book on his recurrent fictional locale.

Like "Packed Dirt," *Olinger Stories* is a "farraginous narrative," composed of a mixture or variety of materials. However, these materials are not confused or jumbled; instead they possess a conscious thematic and imagistic logic. On a smaller and more compressed scale, then, "Packed Dirt" mirrors the structure of *Olinger Stories*, though it seems more composed rather than arranged, with obvious links, such as the repeated motif of the path, embedded to promote coherence. *Olinger Stories*, on the other hand, like the settlement of Fanning Island in "The Blessed Man," relies more on "accidents" as "the generating agency beneath the seemingly achieved surface of things," as we read separately composed stories in a fresh context and construct a new coherence that simultaneously lends Olinger a more tangible existence and endows it with a mythic status.

—Robert M. Luscher, *John Updike: A Study of the Short Fiction* (New York: Twayne Publishers, 1993): pp. 40, 41–42.

Works by
John Updike

The Carpentered Hen and Other Tame Creatures: Poems. 1958.

The Poorhouse Fair. 1959.

The Same Door: Short Stories. 1959.

Rabbit, Run. 1960.

Pigeon Feathers and Other Stories. 1962.

The Magic Flute. Adapted for children from the opera by Mozart. 1962.

The Centaur. 1963.

Telephone Poles and Other Poems. 1963.

Olinger Stories, A Selection. 1964.

The Ring. Adapted for children from the opera cycle by Wagner. 1964.

Assorted Prose. 1965.

Of the Farm. 1965.

A Child's Calendar. 1965.

Verse: The Carpentered Hen and Other Tame Creatures (and) *Telephone Poles and Other Poems.* 1965.

The Music School: Short Stories. 1966.

Bottom's Dream. Adapted from William Shakespeare's *A Midsummer Night's Dream.* 1966.

Couples. 1968.

Bath After Sailing. 1968.

The Angels. 1968.

Three Texts from Early Ipswich. 1968.

On Meeting Authors. 1968.

Midpoint and Other Poems. 1969.

Bech: A Book. 1970.

Rabbit Redux. 1971.

Museums and Women and Other Stories. 1972.

Seventy Poems. 1972.

Warm Wine, An Idyll. 1973.

Six Poems. 1973.

A Good Place. 1973.

Buchanan Dying, A Play. 1974.

Cunts. 1974.

A Month of Sundays. 1975.

Picked-Up Pieces. 1975.

Marry Me: A Romance. 1976.

Couples: A Short Story. 1976.

Tossing and Turning: Poems. 1977.

Hub Fans Bid Kid Adieu. 1977.

The Coup. 1978.

From the Journal of a Leper. 1978.

Too Far to Go: The Maples Stories. 1979.

Problems and Other Short Stories. 1979.

Three Illuminations in the Life of an American Author. 1979.

Sixteen Sonnets. 1979.

Talk from the Fifties. 1979.

The Chaste Planet. 1980.

Ego and Art in Walt Whitman. 1980.

Five Poems. 1980.

People One Knows. 1980.

Rabbit Is Rich. 1981.

Hawthorne's Creed. 1981.

Invasion of the Book Envelopes. 1981.

Bech Is Back. 1982.

The Carpentered Hen. 1982.

The Beloved. 1982.

Spring Trio. 1982.

Hugging the Shore: Essays and Criticism. 1983.

The Witches of Eastwick. 1984.

Emersonianism. 1984.

Confessions of a Wild Bore. 1984.

Jester's Dozen. 1984.

The Best American Short Stories 1984, ed., with Shannon Ravenel. 1984.

Facing Nature: Poems. 1985.

Impressions. 1985.

Getting Older. 1985.

Roger's Version. 1986.

A &P: Lust in the Aisles. 1986.

A Soft Spring Night in Shillington. 1986.

Trust Me. 1987.

Forty Stories. 1987.

The Afterlife. 1987.

More Stately Mansions. 1987.

S. 1988.

Going Abroad. 1988.

On the Move. 1988.

Getting the Words Out. 1988.

Self-Consciousness: Memoirs. 1989.

Just Looking: Essays on Art. 1989.

In Memoriam Felis Felis. 1989.

Rabbit at Rest. 1990.

Brother Grasshopper. 1990.

Recent Poems. 1990.

Mites and Other Poems in Miniature. 1990.

Odd Jobs: Essays and Criticism. 1991.

Thanatopses. 1991.

Memories of the Ford Administration. 1992.

Collected Poems 1953–1993. 1993.

Brazil. 1993.

Concerts at Castle Hill. 1993.

Baby's First Step. 1993.

The Afterlife and Other Stories. 1994.

Golf Dreams: Writings on Golf. 1996.

In the Beauty of the Lilies. 1996.

Down Time. 1997.

Toward the End of Time. 1997.

Bech at Bay: A Quasi-Novel. 1998.

The Best American Short Stories of the Century. Editor. 1999.

Gertrude and Claudius. 2000.

Works about
John Updike

Bloom, Harold, ed. *John Updike.* New York: Chelsea House, 1987.

Burchard, Rachel C. *John Updike: Yea Sayings.* Carbondale: Southern Illinois University Press, 1971.

Campbell, Jeff. *Updike's Novels: Thorns Spell a Word.* Wichita Falls, Texas: Midwestern State University Press, 1987.

Cassidy, Thomas E. "The Enchantment of the Ordinary." *Commonweal* 11 (1959): 499.

Chanley, Steven M. "Quest for Order in 'Pigeon Feathers': Updike's Use of Christian Mythology." *Arizona Quarterly* 43 (1987): 2513.

Cochran, Robert W. "The Narrator Then and Now in Updike's 'Flight.'" *Rendezvous* 10 (Fall 1975): 29–32.

DeBellis, Jack. "Updike: A Selected Checklist 1974–1990." *Modern Fiction Studies* 37 (1991): 129–56.

Dessner, Lawrence Jay. "Irony and Innocence in John Updike's 'A & P.'" *Studies in Short Fiction* 25 (1988): 315–17.

Gearhart, Elizabeth. *John Updike: A Comprehensive Bibliography with Selected Annotations.* Norwood, Pa.: Norwood Press, 1978.

Gingher, Robert S. "Has Updike Anything to Say?" *Modern Fiction Studies* 20 (1974): 95–105.

Greiner, Donald J. "John Updike." *Contemporary Authors: Bibliographical Series.* Vol. 1. Detroit: Gale Research, 1986.

Hamilton, Alice, and Kenneth Hamilton. *John Updike: A Critical Essay.* Grand Rapids, Mich.: William B. Eerdmans, 1967.

Hardwick, Elizabeth. "Citizen Updike." *New York Review of Books* 18 (1989): 3–8.

Hunt, George. *John Updike and the Three Great Things: Sex, Religion, and Art.* Grand Rapids, Mich.: William B. Eerdmans, 1980.

Hurley, C. Harold. "Updike's 'A & P': An 'Initial' Response." *Notes on Contemporary Literature* 20 (1990): 12.

Kinsela, Rebbie. "Pigeon Feathers and Witches." *Christianity Today* 7 (1986): 60.

Luscher, Robert M. "John Updike's *Olinger Stories:* New Light among the Shadows." *Journal of the Short Story in English* 11 (1988): 99–117.

Macnaughton, William R., ed. *Critical Essays on John Updike.* Boston: G. K. Hall, 1982.

Mann, Susan Garland. *The Short Story Cycle: A Genre Companion and Reference Guide.* Westport, Conn.: Greenwood Press, 1988.

Markle, Joyce B. *Fighters and Lovers: Theme in the Novels of John Updike.* New York: New York University Press, 1973.

Meyer, Arlin G., and Michael A. Olivas. "Criticism of John Updike: A Selected Checklist." *Modern Fiction Studies* 20 (1974): 121–33.

Olivas, Michael A. *An Annotated Bibliography of John Updike Criticism 1967–1973, and A Checklist of His Works.* New York: Garland, 1975.

Overall, Nadine. "John Updike's *Olinger Stories:* A Selection." *Studies in Short Fiction* 4 (1967): 195–97.

Peden, William. *The American Short Story: Continuity and Change 1940–1975.* Boston: Houghton Mifflin, 1975.

Pradon, Robert J. "Updike's *Olinger Stories.* In the Middle Landscape Tradition." *Perspectives on Contemporary Literature* 5 (1979): 62–68.

Samuels, Charles Thomas. *John Updike.* Minneapolis: University of Minnesota Press, 1969.

Sokoloff, B. A., and David E. Arnason. *John Updike: A Comprehensive Bibliography.* Norwood, Pa.: Norwood Editions, 1972.

Tallent, Elizabeth. *Married Men and Magic Tricks: John Updike's Erotic Heroes.* Berkeley, Calif.: Creative Arts, 1981.

Taylor, C. Clarke. *John Updike: A Bibliography.* Kent, Ohio: Kent State University Press, 1968.

Thorburn, David, and Howard Eiland, eds. *John Updike: A Collection of Critical Essays.* Englewood Cliffs, N.J.: Prentice Hall, 1979.

Waxman, Robert E. "Invitations to Dread: John Updike's Metaphysical Quest." *Renascence* 29 (1977): 201–10.

Weaver, Gordon, ed. *The American Short Story, 1945–1980. A Critical History.* Boston: Twayne, 1983.

Yates, Morris. "The Doubt and Faith of John Updike." *College English* 26 (1965): 169–74.

Index of
Themes and Ideas

"FLIGHT," 43–60; ambiguity in, 50–53; as autobiographical, 50, 54, 60; Molly Bingaman in, 45, 46–47, 48, 49, 50, 51, 52, 53, 54, 55, 56, 58, 60; characters in, 48; critical views on, 49–60; Allen Dow in, 43–47, 48, 49, 50–51, 52–53, 54, 55–56, 57–59, 60; Allen Dow's grandfather in, 43, 44, 45, 47, 48, 58, 60; Lillian Dow as manipulative in, 53–55; Lillian Dow in, 43, 44, 45, 46, 47, 48, 49, 50, 51–52, 53–56, 57–58, 60, 90; Victor Dow in, 44–45, 46, 48, 51, 53; emotional action of, 57–59; escape and loss images in, 59–60; hyperbole in, 55–56; Judith and Catharine Miller in, 45–46, 48; *Of the Farm* compared to, 49–50, 51; plot summary of, 43–47

"FRIENDS FROM PHILADELPHIA," 10, 33, 37

GERTRUDE AND CLAUDIUS, 12

"HAPPIEST I'VE BEEN, THE," 94

HUGGING THE SHORE, 12

"MOBILE OF BIRDS," 69

MONTH OF SUNDAYS, A, 12

"MUSIC SCHOOL, THE," 12

MUSIC SCHOOL, THE, 95

OF THE FARM, 49–50, 51, 87, 88

OLINGER STORIES: A SELECTION, 43, 78

"PACKED DIRT, CHURCHGOING, A DYING CAT, A TRADED CAR," 78–95; as autobiographical, 91–92; characters in, 84; critical views on, 85–86; family sayings in, 92–93; David Kern in, 75, 78–83, 84, 85–86, 88–91, 93–95; David Kern's religious crisis in, 88–90; Elaine Kern in, 79, 80, 81, 84; Mr. Kern in, 79, 81, 82, 83, 84, 86, 88, 89, 90, 94; Mrs. Kern in, 79, 81, 82, 83, 84, 88, 89; plot summary of, 79–83; supernatural mail in, 85–86; weakness of, 90–91; young sailor in, 81, 84, 89

"PERSISTENCE OF DESIRE, THE," 50

"PIGEON FEATHERS," 61–80; background of, 76–77; characters in, 66; Christianity in, 63–64, 69, 71, 72–74, 76–77, 78; critical views on, 9, 67–80, 88; Reverend M. Dobson in, 63–64, 69; Granmom in, 62, 64, 66; Hebraic-Christian tradition in, 67–68; individual faith in, 72–74; David Kern in, 61, 62–65, 66, 67–68, 69, 70, 72–73, 74–75, 78; Elsie Kern in, 61, 62, 63–64, 65, 66, 67–68, 90; George Kern in, 61, 62, 63, 64, 66, 67; personal mythology in, 74–75; plot summary of, 61–65; proof of God's existence in, 69–71; verbal brilliance of, 71–72